DATE DUE			
10·10·97			
MR 12 '04			

155.9
DIG

DiGiulio, Robert C.

Straight talk about
death and dying

Straight Talk About Death and Dying

Straight Talk About Death and Dying

Robert DiGiulio, Ph.D.
and
Rachel Kranz

■® Facts On File, Inc.
AN INFOBASE HOLDINGS COMPANY

Straight Talk About Death and Dying

Facts on File, Inc.
460 Park Avenue South
New York NY 10016

Library of Congress Cataloging-in-Publication Data

DiGiulio, Robert C., 1949-
Straight talk about death and dying / Robert DiGiulio, Rachel Kranz.
p. cm.
ISBN 0-8160-3078-2 (alk. paper)
1. Death—Psychological aspects—Juvenile literature. I. Kranz, Rachel. II. Title.
BF789.D4D54 1995
155.9'37—dc20   95-2488

Facts on File books are available at special discounts when purchased in bulk quantities for businesses, associations, institutions or sales promotions. Please call our Special Sales Department in New York at 212/683-2244 or 800/322-8755.

Jacket design by Catherine Rincon Hyman

Printed in the United States of America

MP FOF 10 9 8 7 6 5 4 3 2 1

This book is printed on acid-free paper.

Lines from "Do Not Go Gentle Into That Good Night," from *Collected Poems* by Dylan Thomas, published by New Directions Press, New York, © copyright 1952, 1971 by the Trustees for the Copyrights of Dylan Thomas.

Contents

About the Straight Talk About . . . series:

The Straight Talk About . . . books provide young adult readers with the most factual, up-to-date information available. Recognizing that the teen years are a time of growth and transition, the authors aim not to dispense any easy answers or moral judgments but to help young people clarify a number of issues and difficult choices and to consider the consequences of their decisions. Each book is thoroughly indexed and contains a directory of resources.

1

American Attitudes toward Death

Felicia* has always thought of herself as just an ordinary kid. Her family has its share of fights, but basically Felicia, her parents, and her two younger brothers all get along pretty well. Last year, when Felicia was a freshman, she started going to a big high school where she didn't know anybody, and that was difficult, but this year, as a sophomore, she's got a few friends and even a steady boyfriend. This year, too, Felicia is interested in drama, and she was just cast in a big part in the fall play.

Lately, though, Felicia's parents have seemed worried about something, and one day, when Felicia gets home from school, she finds out what it is. Felicia's father takes her aside and explains that her mother is sick. He says that

---

* The teenagers described in these scenarios are *composites*—portraits that combine many different features from various teenagers. Unless noted otherwise, none of them is an actual person.

Felicia's mother will have to quit her job with the phone company and stay at home.

"But just until she gets better, right?" Felicia asks.

"Oh, sure," says her father, but he sounds funny to Felicia. She wonders whether he is telling her the truth. Then he says, "We don't want to worry your mother—or your brothers. I'm telling you because you're the oldest, but don't tell your mother we talked about it, okay? And please don't talk about this with your brothers, your friends, or anybody else. As far as the rest of the world is concerned, your mother is just taking a little time off."

Felicia agrees to do what her father asks her, and outside she seems calm and in control. Inside, though, she's starting to get really scared. All sorts of thoughts and questions are tumbling through her mind. Just how sick is her mother? Will her mother be sick at home, or will she have to go to the hospital? Is she going to get better, or is she going to die? And if she does die, who will take care of Felicia and her brothers? Can her father do it alone? What if it's too much for him? Will he have to marry someone else?

Felicia also thinks of little things. Her mother was going to take her shopping this weekend to get a new winter coat—does this mean they won't go? Her mother does all the cooking—does this mean Felicia will have to do it now? She's ashamed to be worrying about these things when her mother is sick, but she can't help it. Felicia's father seems so upset that she doesn't want to ask him any questions. All she knows is that something really awful must be going on if nobody is supposed to talk about it.

Harry has always had a lot of friends. In fact, each year since he was 5, he has had a different best friend. For the past two years, though, at age 12 and 13, his best friend has been Clem. He and Clem spend a lot of time with their crowd, going to the movies, playing video games, playing soccer and softball. But sometimes he and Clem hang out by themselves, just the two of them. It seems as if he and

Clem can talk about anything. Harry tells Clem things he wouldn't tell anybody else, and he knows Clem has told him secrets too.

One Monday morning when Harry gets to school, he notices that Clem is absent. Harry knew that Clem and his family were going upstate for the weekend to visit Clem's grandfather and that they weren't expected back until late Sunday night. Still, he's surprised not to see his friend in school this morning. He asks the homeroom teacher where Clem is, expecting to hear that Clem is out with the flu or a cold. Instead, the teacher gets this funny look on her face. Then she says, "I'm sorry, Harry. Clem was in an accident this weekend. They took him to the hospital and he died."

Harry is stunned. Clem has been dead all weekend and nobody even told him? He feels like crying, but he doesn't want to cry in front of the teacher and his other classmates. He feels like screaming, or breaking something, or running so fast and so far that he could get away from this awful feeling, but his teacher is saying "I'm so sorry, Harry—but you'd better get to class now, you don't want to be late."

Harry feels like a zombie. He goes to his next class, but he still can't believe what he heard. Maybe the teacher was just playing a trick on him, he thinks. Or maybe she got the wrong information. She didn't even tell him much about the accident—he at least wants to know what happened. During the break in his next class, he tries to find a phone to call Clem's house, but students aren't allowed to use the phone in the office except in an emergency, and the secretary doesn't think this is an emergency. "This can wait till you get home," she says.

After school, Harry races home. His father is already there. "Did you hear what happened to Clem?" Harry asks. "Is it true?" His father hasn't heard anything, and when Harry tells him the news, he tries to discourage Harry from calling Clem's family. "This is a time for family to be alone together," he tells Harry. "It's not a time for outsiders to be bothering them."

Harry can't believe what he's hearing. He's not an outsider—he's Clem's best friend! Doesn't anybody understand what this means to him?

Carmen is shopping with her friends at the mall one Saturday afternoon when she first hears the news. It seems that a guy in their class, Josh Silverman, committed suicide by hanging himself from a tree in the schoolyard. The death was so dramatic that it made it onto the 24-hour news radio station, and one of the girls working at the mall heard it at work. She told Carmen and her friends, and pretty soon, the news is all over the mall.

Carmen feels terrible. She barely knew Josh—there are more than 300 people in the senior class of Carmen's big-city school—but somehow, just the idea of someone killing himself makes her feel terrible. She remembers the one or two times she spoke to Josh, when she ran into him in the library or the one time he was in her biology class. She thinks she remembers how lonely he looked, how he always wanted to be friendly. "Maybe if I had been more friendly to him, he wouldn't have done what he did," she thinks.

She tries to say something nice about Josh to her friends, but to her surprise, they don't see it that way at all. "Look, the guy was *weird*," Eileen says. "Who else would do something so crazy?"

"Actually, I think it was kind of mean of him to do it right at the school like that," says Linda. "How are we supposed to go in there now? We'll just always be thinking about it. Couldn't he have picked someplace else?"

"Maybe he just wanted the attention," Miriam says. "Well, it didn't work, 'cause *I* barely remember him anyway."

Now Carmen feels worse than ever. She feels bad about Josh, and she's upset that her friends are so unfeeling. She starts wondering why she's so upset when nobody else seems to be. Why is she always so different from everybody? She doesn't want her friends to know how different, so she doesn't say anything more. But that night, when she's getting ready for bed, she finds herself feeling scared and jumpy, worried that something might be just outside the window, thinking she hears noises in the hallway and in her sister's room next door. And she has bad dreams about Josh all night.

Coming to Terms with Death

Throughout history, humans have struggled to come to terms with one undeniable fact: At the end of our lives, we each must die. And throughout our lives, it is virtually certain that someone we love will die before we do, leaving us alive to mourn and grieve that person's death.

Different cultures have handled this inescapable fact in different ways. Some cultures are very close to death. For much of human history, *infant mortality* rates were very high. That means that of all the children born, many may not have lived to see their fifth birthdays. Likewise, until the 20th century, women frequently died in childbirth, sometimes as many as one woman in three. Accidents, famine, diseases, and the generally difficult conditions of life meant that *life expectancy* was short—that many men and women were likely to die by the time they were 40 or 50—an early death, by our standards. And since in these cultures, sick and dying people were cared for by their families, children grew up in a world that included both healthy people and sick ones, both people in the prime of life and people who were dying.

Today many cultures still operate under some or all of these conditions: a high rate of infant mortality, a high rate of women's death in childbirth, a relatively short life expectancy, a pattern of caring for the sick and dying at home rather than in institutions. Although people in these cultures mourn their losses too, they aren't shocked by the fact of death itself. From a very early age, children are likely to witness the deaths of people they know—a younger brother or sister, a grandparent or a parent, a neighbor or friend. Children in rural cultures also are likely to witness the killing of farm animals or the hunting of wild animals for food or clothing, seeing for themselves that death is constantly present in the midst of life—that death is sometimes even necessary to *preserve* life.

In our own society, on the other hand, economic, social, and medical advances have made death at an early age much less common. In most regions of the United States, the infant mortality rate is relatively low, meaning that most—though not all—children who are born live to grow up. (In the 1980s, however, infant mortality rates rose sharply in some communities, particularly poor African-American and Latino communities in big cities.) At the same time, women's survival rate in childbirth is very high, meaning that very few women die giving birth. People tend to live longer, which means that young children are less likely to know people who have died. And since most sick, dying, and elderly people are cared for by hospitals, nursing homes, and other institutions, children and adults are far less likely to come into contact with people who are close to death.

As a result, death in American culture has become a kind of unspeakable subject, something that many people find difficult to talk about. Children and teenagers dealing with the deaths or illnesses of people they care about may not know anyone else who has died, making the experience even more strange and difficult than it would be anyway. Worse, they may live in communities where the adults are not familiar with death either, making it difficult for anyone to understand what a child or teenager might be going through when he or she confronts the death or illness of a parent, friend, relative, or acquaintance.

Mainstream American culture may contribute to this sense of isolation, for it has tended to focus on youth, health, beauty, and fitness, particularly in the 1980s and 1990s. The dominant culture, ignoring or suppressing our Native American heritage, has always portrayed the United States as a "young" country, as if it began when the first European settlers came here in the 17th century. This image of youth has become increasingly important since the 1950s, when the idea of the "youth culture" first attained prominence. Today young people's music, fashions, and media idols dominate much of our culture. Advertisements tell people what beauty products to buy to look young, what beverages to drink to think young, and what products to purchase to "live young." Images of aging, dying, and sickness may seem bizarre and unnatural, rather than an expected and inevitable part of all our lives.

Not all cultures value youth in this way. The Chinese, for example, traditionally have seen old age as the crowning glory of a life—a time to sit back and enjoy the respect of the community and an opportunity to exercise one's power over younger members of the family. Native Americans also see the elderly as the keepers of wisdom and tradition, valued guides for the rest of the nation, teachers and shamans who can initiate younger people into the tribe's ways. In these cultures, aging, sickness, and death have a place that is familiar to everyone. A child or teenager would be far more likely to see death as something to be expected—however painful and unwelcome—and that young person's grief would be far more likely to be recognized and given a place in his or her community.

Helping Children Respond to Death

When we think about the difficulty that our society generally has in dealing with aging, sickness, and death, we can understand more easily why so many people have trouble helping children, in particular, respond to death. Which of the following statements sound familiar to you, as expressing attitudes that many people have about children's responses to death? Do you think these attitudes are helpful to children or not?

- "Your father has died, but don't cry. He would want you to be a big, strong boy and take it like a man."
- "Your mother has gone away on a trip. You won't see her again for a long, long time."
- "You're too young to go to the funeral."
- "Your brother was such a good person that God just decided He wanted him up in heaven—so don't be sad."
- "Death is just like going to sleep—except the dead person doesn't wake up."
- "Your grandmother is up in heaven now, where she can watch everything you do."
- "I know you're sad that your friend has died, but you'll get over it. You have so many other friends."
- "How can you make so much noise? Don't you *care* that Aunt Ella has died?"
- "Your grandpa has been dead for two days now, and you haven't cried once. What's the matter? Don't you love him?"
- "Your mother is in heaven now, so there's no reason for you to feel sad."

As you might have thought, statements such as these are generally *not* helpful to children. That's because all of them are based on attitudes that seek to deny the nature of death—its finality and the pain it brings to the survivors. In a culture where death's reality is ignored or suppressed, it's all too easy to ask children to participate in that process, encouraging them to ignore or suppress their own responses to death.

Hence the wish of many adults wish to keep children away from funerals. Of course, some children really may be too young to attend a funeral, and others genuinely may prefer not to go. Many children and teenagers, however, have said they found it helpful to attend a funeral or memorial service and that such ceremonies helped them to accept the reality of the person's death and to draw comfort from the presence of other people who loved the deceased person. Even when a goldfish or a pet kitten dies, having a funeral and a burial service can be helpful, a way of coming to terms with the loss of a loved creature. Yet frequently adults will not even discuss the prospect of any type of funeral, wake, or service with bereaved children, particularly if they were not close relatives of the person who died.

Other statements on the list simply distort the reality of death, in ways that often frighten or confuse children. For example, to tell a child that death is like a long trip might lead the child to wonder when the dead person is coming back and why the person chose to leave. In her book *Learning to Say Good-bye: When a Child's Parent Dies*, Eda LeShan tells the story of her mother, who lost her own mother when she was only four years old. For a long time, the grown-ups let that four-year-old child believe that her mother was just away on a trip. The little girl concluded that her mother had left because she was angry with her. She felt that she must have been very bad to cause her mother to go away for so long. How much better would it have been, LeShan writes, if someone could have told that little girl the truth. As painful as it might have been to understand that she would never see her mother again, it would have been less painful than believing that her mother had chosen to go away. We can only speculate the extent to which the American discomfort with death had something to do with the need of those grown-ups to distort death's reality.

Likewise, to tell a child that death is like sleep is not helpful, because the child knows that he or she goes to sleep every night. Is there then a chance that he or she might never wake up? What about the other beloved people that child sees sleeping? Will they perhaps one day not wake up? Explaining death as its own reality is less frightening to a child. But in order to talk about death accurately, an adult must be comfortable with at least the *idea* of death, seeing it as a natural part of life and not as a taboo subject that cannot be talked about.

By the same token, telling a child that God wanted a "good" person up in heaven may be frightening; such an explanation might easily lead the child to fear that his or her being "good" will lead to death, or that God will soon want other good people—other parents, relatives, or friends—in heaven too. A child also might be frightened at the idea that a "grandmother in heaven can see everything you do" because the child could easily picture an angry or judgmental person monitoring "bad" actions and thoughts. Both of these explanations, which seek to make death easier for the child, are actually a way of denying its reality: that the dead person has gone and is not coming back.

Another type of denial might lead to telling a child that "Your mother is in heaven now, so there's no reason for you to feel sad." Although one may believe in heaven or in an afterlife, telling a child to "not feel sad" because of that belief denies an important reality of death—the child's pain at a terrible loss. Even if the child is not close to the person or pet that has died, the child may still feel great grief at the loss. Trying to deny a painful and sad reality can be confusing and upsetting to a child who needs to know that it's all right to grieve. "Why does God need our mother?" one bereaved father remembers his young daughter asking. "We need her more, right here!"

In the same vein, the well-meaning but misguided people who might tell a child not to cry are part of a cultural pattern that seeks to deny death and minimize its power to affect us. Both adults and children are often expected to carry on "as if nothing had happened," even after losing a parent, a child, a spouse, or an intimate friend. Cultures that do not deny the reality of death seem to have an easier time accepting people's needs to grieve and mourn.

On the other hand, the people who wonder how a child can be noisy and playful after a death, or why he or she doesn't cry, need to understand that each child—and each teenager, and each adult—grieves a death in his or her own way. There is no "right" time to cry: Some people react more quickly with tears, others cry only after the worst hurt has passed or after the initial shock has worn off. Every person grieves in his or her own way. Eda LeShan tells the story of a man who lost his father when he was a little boy. He tried to think of what he could do to show his love for his father, and he came up with the idea of finishing a woodworking project his father had left uncompleted. He felt proud of himself for doing something he believed his father would have wanted—but his mother, who didn't understand, scolded him for making noise and "playing" in the wood shop so soon after his father's death.

As you can see, our culture's fears and anxieties about death affect the way we deal with children when someone they love has died. But children also bring their own abilities and limitations to the problem of death. How much can they understand about this difficult topic?

Children's Views of Death

In *Don't Take My Grief Away: What to Do When You Lose a Loved One,* Doug Manning writes, *"Children feel, even if they do not understand. Understanding comes later—the feelings need a hug."* As he explains, one of the most difficult aspects of death for children is that while they are aware of the loss of a loved one, they may not have the intellectual ability to understand what death means. Most children cannot really understand death the way adults understand it until they are teenagers.

Yet regardless of their intellectual ability to grasp the meaning of death, children of all ages are deeply affected by the loss of a parent. Until they become teenagers, and sometimes even then, children's main sense of themselves comes from their parents. It's through their parents' responses that they understand both *who* they are ("Look at this handsome little boy!" "Did you make this picture? You must be an artist!" "Wendy's quite an athlete—look at her climb to the top of that tree!") and *how good* they are ("Thank you for playing so quietly while I was sick." "I'm very angry with you for breaking my favorite vase." "You're being such a good helper today!").

Children also pick up a great deal from their parents' *nonverbal* responses—a smile, a frown, a hug, a shake of the head. After all, how else can children learn? It's only by a parent's response that a two-year-old can understand that it's fine to mix mud and water in the backyard, but not to mix flour and water on the kitchen floor. How else can a five-year-old learn the the difference between tying a shoelace and tying a knot? And without a parent's reaction, how would a seven-year-old know that a pink-and-purple striped shirt might not be the best choice to put on with green-and-yellow polka-dot pants? It's only by a parent's response that a child can learn that people like to be hugged and kissed, but they don't like to be hit or bitten, or that being cheerful and polite seems to make people happy while being grouchy or rude seems to make them mad.

Of course, the responses of other people—beloved adults, brothers and sisters, friends—count too. But until they become teenagers, most children take their parents' responses as the main indicator of how they're doing in the world.

That's why the loss of a parent is so devastating to a child. To a child, especially a very young child, losing a parent feels like losing the world. Even adults have a hard time giving up a person who was an important *part* of their world. But a child who loses Mommy or Daddy feels like his or her *whole* world is gone.

Along with coping with the loss of a beloved person, a child will want to understand what has happened to him or her and want some reassurance that it won't happen again. This understanding will vary, depending on the child's age. Children's ability to understand death changes as they grow older, until age 13 or so, when they are intellectually able to understand death as well as an adult. Therefore, it's helpful for adults and teenagers to realize just how much preteenage children can and can't understand.

Children Age Two and Younger

Very young children have no idea of death whatsoever. What they do understand, though, is that their parents and the people around them are upset. These children need comfort just as much as or more than the older people who may have a better understanding of what has occurred. If a child's parents are unhappy and upset, the child also will feel unhappy and unsettled, and it's important that others comfort or reassure the child, even in the midst of their own grief.

Even though young children don't understand death, they do understand separation. If the person who has died is someone who takes care of the child, the child may miss that person without being able to say or even understand that he or she is experiencing a loss. When children lose parents at this young age, their pain is especially intense, since it's impossible for them to comprehend what has happened. All they know is that someone they love isn't there any more. These children particularly need to be held and touched, especially by people they know, such as the surviving parent or grandparents.

Children Ages Three to Five

Children of this age are aware that something bad has happened, but they don't understand death itself. They do have a sense of their own bodies, so they can imagine being mutilated or hurt. They could grasp the concept of being "all smashed up," or "cut up into little pieces," or even "very, very sick," but they can't grasp the *permanence* of death.

Children of this age group need to be supported by and feel safe with a loving adult, even if it is a parent who has died. As children grow, and as time passes, they will gradually accept death as permanent. But this acceptance cannot be speeded up. Some children may continue to save a place in their lives for that missing person, but this does not mean that they are unable to grow close to people who really are available. That's why, even for very young children, it might be helpful for them to be allowed to view the body or at least to attend the funeral: It may help make the child's growing understanding of the permanence of death easier to grasp. Even adults have trouble grasping death's permanence on an emotional level, so it is easy to imagine how much harder this is for a child who can't understand it intellectually either.

Another difficulty for children of this age can be their feelings of guilt and fear about causing the death. Since children this age are still sorting out the difference between their wishes and reality, they may be prey to "magical thinking"—the idea that something happened just because they wanted it to.

This springs from their early experiences as infants. When a baby is very small and he or she cries, an adult usually appears, bringing food, dry diapers, or some other form of comfort. The baby doesn't understand that the grown-ups came of their will, because of their own understanding of a baby's cry and their own wish to help. To the baby, it seems as if his or her wish "made" the grown-up appear. As the baby gets older, he or she will continue to think that his or her wishes have the power to make things happen in the world.

Thus, when angry at a parent or sibling, a young child may "wish they were dead," not in any real way—remember, they don't understand that death is permanent—but as a temporary burst of anger. They may feel that, just as the wish to be fed made a parent appear, their anger at a parent made the parent disappear.

Of course, children don't *really* wish their parents were dead. They don't understand death as a permanent state. They may just want an annoying parent to disappear *for a little while.* As Elisabeth Kübler-Ross writes in her book *Living with Death and Dying,* a young child might hear Mommy say "No!" and immediately wish she was dead—that is, gone, somewhere where she *can't* say no. The next minute, though, that child wishes Mommy were right there, making him a peanut-butter sandwich for lunch. Or a child might wish that a bossy older brother would just *go away*—until five minutes later, when he wants to play with his big brother again. And if the parent or sibling of a young child actually does die, the child remembers wishing he or she would "die" and feels guilty and afraid, worrying that perhaps these "bad" wishes somehow made the death happen.

Of course, an adult or an older child can understand that bad wishes don't hurt anybody—you have to *act* on your wishes before they have any impact in the world. And, hopefully, an adult or teenager can also understand that we all occasionally feel angry, envious, or resentful of the people we love—those feelings are just part of a relationship and nothing to be ashamed of. (However, it takes most adults years to *really* understand these two things, because we all have "baby" feelings inside us too!)

A young child, however, sees the whole world in terms of him- or herself. When someone beloved dies, a young child is apt to really believe it was his or her fault. Children of this age will have particular difficulty accepting the death of a parent or sibling with whom they had a troubled relationship—say, an abusive or frequently absent parent. The angrier the child was at the parent while the parent was alive, the more guilty and frightened the child is likely to feel after the parent has died, causing the child to worry that his or her anger might have caused the parent's death.

So the second challenge for children of this age is to understand that they were not responsible for the death of the loved one. Children this age (and older) need help in understanding this, by talking with parents or other sympathetic adults, with older brothers and sisters, or sometimes with a professional counselor or therapist. (See Chapter 6.)

Children Ages Six to Eight

Children of this age experience many of the problems younger children have when they face a death. They sense that, with the loss of a parent, their whole world and their whole identity has been shaken. They may also have difficulty grasping the permanence of death, and feel guilty over their imaginary responsibility for the event. Since children of this age are old enough to be more aware of their feelings—anger with a bossy older sister, envy of a babied younger brother, resentment at a father who lives somewhere else, frustration with a mother who leaves every day to go to work—they also may keenly feel the kinds of conflicts we've described. They may be especially likely to feel guilty or frightened that their "bad feelings" were somehow responsible for the death of the person they were mad at or jealous of.

However, at this age, children are better able to ask questions and to explain their thoughts. The challenge for children this age is to find the grown-ups who can answer their questions and, to the best of their ability, help them understand what has happened.

As we have seen, this need is often frustrated by adults' own discomfort with death. Adults who try to respond to a child's questions by saying "God has taken your mommy away" or "Death is like going to sleep," may, without meaning to, create more confusion and pain for the child. Also, children of this age often are fascinated by ghosts, skeletons, and monsters—figures that they associate with their shadowy understanding of death. Therefore, although

children of this age are still limited in what they can understand, they nevertheless need clear explanations of a situation rather than being left to form their own conclusions. Indeed, the presence of a loving adult, as well as the openness that adult feels toward the child's questions, will go far in helping the child deal with loss.

Some children are not, by nature, talkative. A quiet child this age also may be misunderstood because he or she seems not to care about a death, especially at first. Adults around such a child may be misled into thinking either that the child doesn't care about the person who died or that the child has found ways of handling his or her grief—or even that the child is "too young to understand" and therefore too young to feel bad.

In fact, adults are much stronger than children, so they may be able to feel more emotion more quickly. A bereaved adult is likely to understand, on some level, that no matter how painful the loss, his or her world will continue. If nothing else, a bereaved parent is likely to know that he or she must carry on "for the sake of the children." Knowing that their world will continue, adults can afford to give way to their grief more easily.

Children, on the other hand, may not be able to feel so much all at once. They may need a day or a week or even several weeks to reassure themselves that their world has *not* fallen apart before they can afford to experience their pain and loss. They may cry a lot at little things because they can't yet face the reality of the loss. They may get upset at other deaths—say, the killing of a fly with a flyswatter, or the war they're reading about in history class—while seeming not to care about the death of the person they loved.

Furthermore, to children of this age, adults are still all-powerful. It's very difficult for a child to believe that any adult does anything without intending to do so. Children may be overwhelmed with anger at the thought of a parent or loved one "leaving" them by dying. It's hard for a child of this age to grasp the reality that the dying person couldn't help "leaving." (Children whose parents committed suicide may have an especially difficult time understanding what happened, since these adults *did* die by choice. It may take years for these children to understand that their parents died because of problems they couldn't handle, not because of anything the child did to make them want to leave.)

The second challenge for children of this age is to understand that the person who died didn't leave "on purpose" and then to find a way to feel their sadness along with their anger. Children of this age need lots of reassurance from adults to know that it's safe to cry and to feel bad about a death as well as to know that it's safe to be angry, even with the person who died.

Children Ages Nine to Twelve

At this age, children are more likely to understand the permanence of death but may have periods where this idea is still a little shaky. John S. Stephenson, in his book *Death, Grief, and Mourning: Individual and Social Realities,* quotes the founder of psychoanalysis, Sigmund Freud, who reports the following statement from a 10-year-old boy: "I know Father's dead, but what I can't understand is why he doesn't come home for dinner." According to Stephenson and Freud, this boy's problem is not so much that he can't grasp the permanence of death intellectually, but that he has trouble accepting the fact emotionally. His way of defending himself against a painful reality is to believe something that isn't true: that his dead father might, indeed, be able to come back and have dinner with them.

David A. Crenshaw, writing in *Bereavement: Counseling the Grieving throughout the Life Cycle,* agrees that children from ages 9 to 12 may still somehow think that death is "reversible." Part of that belief, he thinks, surfaces because children of this age are just beginning to understand that they too can die. If someone they know dies—particularly a sibling or someone close to their age—it reinforces the frightening thoughts about their own death.

These thoughts may be especially painful because, according to psychologist Erik Erikson, this is the age where children are trying to figure out how useful and powerful they are in the world. Finding out that they may be powerless to prevent their own death or the death of someone they love is especially upsetting.

Children of this age are just figuring out how much they can do in the world, getting ready for that bigger measure of power and independence they'll move into as teenagers. Losing a parent may be especially hard at this age because just as children are figuring out where they *don't* need their parents ("I can do my homework by myself!" "Now I can fix my own lunch!"), death comes along to remind them how much they *do* need their parents ("I still need help with the math." "Who will make me dinner?").

The challenge for children of this age, then, is to find a way to accept their powerlessness in the face of death while realizing that they may be powerful and effective in many other areas. They also may need to let themselves "feel like babies" for a while—after all, the death of a loved one makes *everyone* feel powerless and babylike for a while, no matter how old or grown-up they are.

Facing a death may be especially hard for children of this age because they are in fact old enough to be relied upon. It's reasonable to ask these preteenagers to help more around the house, to do some baby-sitting of other siblings, or to be polite and gracious while staying with relatives or friends—all of which may be necessary in the period after someone has died. At the same time, these children might get the message that they're not allowed to be sad or angry, that the grown-ups' grief and mourning is more important than theirs. David Crenshaw points out that children of this age who don't give any sign of mourning may feel that it's their job to be "strong" for their parents. So another challenge for children of this age faced with a death is to "rise to the occasion" while also getting space to cry, to be mad, or just to feel bad.

Teenagers and Death

What about teenagers? What special problems might they face in dealing with death? We'll look at those issues more closely at the beginning of Chapter 2. First, however, let's take one more look at the particular ways that our society and some others handle death. Knowing some of the ways that people deal with this universal human experience may help you to develop your own ideas about how to pass through grief and mourning, so that when your time comes to confront someone's death, you'll have more ways of getting support for your feelings.

How Different Cultures Confront Death

As we saw earlier, in most traditional cultures, death is a much more visible and constant presence in people's lives. Consequently, these cultures tend to have elaborate rituals dealing with death. In these cultures, children and adults alike become, if not accepting of death, at least familiar with it. It may always be a shock when a loved one gets sick or dies, but it is a kind of familiar shock, something to be expected as much as growing up, getting married, or having children.

In some Native American cultures, for example, hunters would say a prayer before killing an animal, acknowledging that they were ending another life to extend their own. And in virtually all cultures, until very recently, people followed specific ceremonies for funerals as well as for the mourning period after a death.

Customs of dealing with death vary from culture to culture. In one society, people might wear black to show their grief at death. In another culture, white might be the color of mourning. Some societies observed other restrictions, such as no dancing for a year or not leaving the house for a week. People might have rules about when they could marry again, or when they could invite guests over. All of these rules were designed to help people make it through the difficult period after the death of a loved one, acknowledging that this is a special time during which it's hard for people to function normally. People in all cultures need time to adjust to life without a loved one and need to mark the importance of a person's life through rituals of grief and mourning.

The disadvantage of these rituals was that they insisted that everyone respond the same way. Perhaps a particular person might be ready to dance and have a good time again in only nine months—but if the rule was "No dancing for a year," that rule would have to be observed. Or perhaps a person might want to invent his or her own way of mourning a loved one who had died, but the society might look sternly on any deviation from the prescribed ritual.

On the other hand, the advantage of these rituals was that they acknowledged the importance of grief and mourning, taking some of the burden off individual mourners by giving them clear guidelines about when to mourn—and when it was all right to stop mourning. In our individualistic culture, people have to figure many more things out for themselves. This may be a good thing, allowing for more choice and more freedom, but it also can be difficult, creating loneliness and uncertainty.

In *Beyond Widowhood*, Dr. Robert DiGiulio wrote about a terrible fire in California that claimed the lives of 17 people of Samoan heritage in 1964. Researchers who were familiar with disasters like this expected the survivors to be devastated to an extent that went beyond more usual reactions to death. After all, this was a sudden, unexpected catastrophe that affected an entire community. In a similar fire in Boston in 1942, survivors had experienced acute grief, shock, and despair.

Yet a researcher studying the Samoan-American community found that its members handled the tragedy extremely well. In fact, when she spoke to them about the reaction of the Boston survivors, the Samoan Americans were surprised at the Bostonians' difficulties. What could explain these different reactions?

The researcher realized that the difference lay in the extent to which the *community as a whole* was able to rally itself in support. The Samoan Americans, for example, immediately gathered at the homes of the bereaved. They took over the management of the household, caring for the children and teenagers who survived and freeing adult survivors from their daily routines while reminding them that they did not have to face this tragedy alone. Other traditional Samoan customs, such as ritual exchanges of food and money, reinforced the idea that there was a supportive network of people that could help each family with its grief. Because no one had to suffer alone, everyone could suffer less.

You may have heard the expression "It takes a village to raise a child." To us, it means that, while family is extremely important, by itself it cannot provide enough support for young people to grow and learn. Other adults and young people must be available to us, providing us with a sense of community that can sustain us when our individual families run into problems. In a sense, this saying applies to death and dying as well. Perhaps it would be accurate to say "It takes a village to mourn a death"—that individuals and families need the support of a community in figuring out how to cope with the loss of a loved one.

Of course, even in the contemporary United States and Canada, many rituals of grief and mourning survive. Do any of the following sound familiar to you? Can you think of others?*

---

*For the information on various cultures' responses to death, we are indebted to *The Seasons of Grief: Helping Children Grow Through Loss*, by Dr. Donna A. Gaffney.

- In traditional Jewish practice, a family sits *shiva* for a week after a death. That means that the family stays at home and receives visitors who traditionally bring food so that the family is freed from the daily routines of cooking. The first meal after the funeral—which is always held as soon as possible—is known as the "Meal of Consolation." Traditionally, mourners tore their clothes; today they often wear a piece of torn cloth pinned to their shirts to signify their sadness. They're also supposed to sit on furniture that's lower to the ground than normal. Further signs of grief include men not shaving and women not wearing makeup. A year after the death, the headstone of the person's tomb is unveiled in another ceremony, marking this important anniversary. The children—traditionally, the sons—say a special prayer, called *Kaddish,* on each anniversary of a parent's death, and families burn *yahrzeit* or memorial candles each year as well.
- Catholic cultures honor the dead with special masses, both in the period immediately after the death and in the months or years afterward. Individuals also may burn special candles at church altars in memory of a loved one, again, either soon after the death or at a later period. In Irish Catholic culture, a huge party, known as a *wake,* is held, reminding the community that we can celebrate life while we mourn death. The party traditionally is held in the same room where the dead person was displayed in his or her open coffin. Some Italian communities have a similar "celebration" after a death. Friends and families in Latino cultures also tend to gather at the funeral, or afterward, openly weeping and wailing to show their grief.
- African Americans in various denominations often come together in church-based communities to commemorate a death. A minister and other church officials often lead funeral services in which the entire congregation participates, providing strong community support for the fam-

ily. Music and singing are often an important part of these services, because they provide comfort and emotional release. Indeed, traditionally, in New Orleans funerals, a brass band marches through the streets, playing jazz to celebrate the person's passage to heaven and also to celebrate the lives of those left on earth.

- Fundamentalists believe that a person who has died is to be judged by God, who decides whether the person should go to heaven or hell. Fundamentalist ministers, speaking to the entire congregation, will therefore recount a person's good deeds at a funeral service. This serves two purposes: It helps puts the family into a supportive community, and it makes the importance of the person's life clear, both for the good deeds he or she did while alive and also to provide an example for the rest of the community. In other words, the service marks the importance of the deceased person's life, which helps loved ones to accept his or her death.

If you are currently mourning the death of a loved one, you might want to think about which rituals you, your family, and your friends might engage in or create as a way of publicly marking the person's importance to you. Of course, mourning and grieving are very private experiences. Yet they also can—and must—be shared. Finding ways to engage your family and your community in a shared ritual might help all of you ease your grief.

Coping with Death

The fact is that all our lives are fragile: Someday we will die, and before we die, we are likely to face the deaths of others whom we love. Many aspects of American culture may seek to deny this fact, but it's true all the same.

In this book, we'll attempt to help you cope with death and dying, as you think about these painful topics and as you or your friends may experience them in your own lives. In the next chapter, we'll look at why coping with death is especially challenging for teenagers, as they move from childhood into adulthood. In Chapter 3, "Coping with Dying," we'll talk about the experience of living with someone who is dying, helping you to better understand that person's experience as well as your own. In Chapter 4, "Coping with Death," we'll explore the ways that a death can affect you, starting from when you first hear the news and continuing through the first year or two after the death. Chapter 5, "Death and Relationships," looks at the particular ways in which a teenager might be affected by the death of a parent, a sibling, and a friend. Finally, in Chapter 6, we'll tell you how to find help in coping with death as well as explain what kinds of help are available. Chapter 7 includes hot lines, addresses, and other resources that you might find helpful.

"Suffering!" wrote the French novelist and essayist Anatole France. "We owe to it all that is good in us, all that gives value to life; we owe to it pity, we owe to it courage, we owe to it all the virtues." It is possible to take the suffering that comes from surviving a loved one's death and turn it into much "that is good in us." It is our goal to suggest a path through the stages of grief and mourning toward that end.

2

Teenagers' Experiences with Death

Felicia is surprised by how quickly her family seems to adjust to her mother's illness. They set up a bed for her in the downstairs den, and during the day, a nurse comes in to help take care of her and leave dinner waiting for the family. She leaves at 4 o'clock, though, when Felicia and her brothers get home from school. Felicia is in charge until 6:30, when her father gets home. Her father speaks to each of the children privately, assigning them a household chore that their mother once did, and then tells Felicia to make sure that her brothers do their chores. For the first month or so, they're pretty good about doing what they're supposed to.

Nobody really talks about the changes, but one day Felicia's father tells her that he's really proud of the way she's taken over for her mother. "I knew I could count on you to fill in," he says. Felicia feels very mixed up hearing him say that. On the one hand, she's proud that her father is proud of her. On the other hand, she's angry and confused. Does this mean she's supposed to do everything her mother used to do? Does her father think she even *could* do that? She doesn't think she could—and even if she could, she doesn't want to. She's not ready to be in charge of a whole house, and she doesn't want to spend that much time taking care of her brothers!

Then Felicia feels guilty. Of course, if her family needs her, she'd have to be a pretty awful person not to even *want* to help out. But maybe she really is an awful person, because she *doesn't* want her whole life to change just because her mother is sick. She wants her life to be the way it was before. She knows it's selfish to feel that way, when her mother is so sick, her father is so worried, and her brothers are even younger and more helpless than she is. But she can't help it. She wants things to be the way they were before.

For a whole week after Clem's death, Harry continues to feel like a zombie. To everybody else, he may look normal, but inside, he feels as if he's just watching the rest of the world on television with the sound turned down. They can hear each other and they all seem to be having a good time together, but he can't reach them and they can't reach him. He's just alone, frozen, too numb to feel anything.

Harry's mother is friends with Clem's mother, and the next day she finds out how the accident happened. At first, she doesn't want to tell Harry because she thinks the details will frighten or upset him. But for once Harry comes out of his zombie state and insists on hearing what happened.

It seems the family was out driving late on a rainy night on a dark country road. Somehow the car skidded and fishtailed, and its back end hit a tree. Clem's sister, who was sitting next to him in the backseat, was shaken up, but for some reason Clem was knocked unconscious. It took them a long time to flag down another car and get Clem to the hospital, and when he got there, the doctor said there was probably nothing he could do. Clem died a few hours later.

When Harry hears what happened, he's so angry, he feels as if he's burning up. He's furious with Clem's parents for taking the car out in such dangerous circumstances. He's enraged that the doctor at the hospital didn't try harder to save his friend. He's even angry with Clem's sister for hogging the best seat—why couldn't it have been her instead of Clem who died?

After a week, Harry's anger and numbness start to wear off and he just feels drained. Every night he cries himself to sleep. He's ashamed of himself—he knows he's too old to cry, and besides, he's a guy. But he can't help it. As soon as the lights go out, he'll find himself remembering something Clem said or did, or he'll catch himself thinking "I'll have to tell Clem about that tomorrow," and then he remembers that there is no Clem anymore. Harry has heard that crying is supposed to make you feel better, but that doesn't work for him. It just makes him think that there must be something really wrong with him to be so upset. After all, as everybody keeps saying, Clem was just his friend. He can make other friends. What's the big deal?

Harry starts to think that he should be very careful in the future. Obviously, no one else thinks he should be this upset over Clem. Next time he makes a friend, he shouldn't let the person become very important to him. That way, the next time a friend dies, Harry can *really* feel the way everybody seems to think he should feel now, instead of just pretending to be okay. Besides, if he doesn't have another best friend, then he can't lose another best friend, and he won't ever have to hurt so much again.

All weekend, Carmen thinks about Josh and his suicide. She wonders what he was thinking when he did it. She wonders whether she could have stopped him, if she had been more friendly, if she had been his friend or even his girlfriend. She wonders whether anyone would notice if *she* felt like killing herself, and whether people would talk about her as casually and mockingly as her friends talked about Josh. It just seems so sad to her that a person is dead and nobody seems to care.

When she gets to school on Monday morning, she looks at the tree in the schoolyard where Josh hanged himself. There's a whole group of kids crowded around it, looking at it, touching it, making jokes. Carmen is mad that they're not showing more respect. There should be something to mark the place, she thinks, a plaque on the tree or something to remind everybody of what happened, so nothing like it will ever happen again. Looking at the tree and the group of kids standing around it, she's surprised to find that she feels like crying. What's the matter with her? After all, she didn't even know Josh!

Carmen knows better than to bring the subject up with her friends again, but to her surprise, they can't stop talking about it. Miriam says a guy told her that a whole branch of the tree just withered and fell off after they found Josh's body and cut it down. She says you can't even see where the branch used to be. "Like it was Josh's ghost or something," she says, "that took away the branch." Carmen doesn't believe this—she doesn't believe in ghosts—but it gives her a creepy feeling to hear it anyway.

"I heard that his mother had a nervous breakdown and now she's in the hospital," Linda says. "I bet *my* mom wouldn't have a breakdown if she knew *I* killed myself. She'd just say, 'Good, one less kid to worry about.'"

Eileen giggles. "My sisters would be like, 'Can I have her room?' 'No, I want it!' 'No, I do.' And then when they were done fighting about my room, they'd start fighting about my clothes."

Carmen tries to act casual, the way they are. "You guys are so sympathetic," she says. "What if it was me?"

"Oh, you," Miriam says. "You would never do anything so stupid, Carmen, so don't even worry about it."

But Eileen takes her seriously. "Don't you *ever* even *think* of doing anything like that!" she says fiercely. "I would be so mad at you I'd bring you back to life and kill you all over again!"

Everybody laughs. But Carmen feels a little bit better. At least somebody would care if she died. She wouldn't be like Josh, gone without a trace.

Teenage Life and Death

As we saw in Chapter 1, children have a range of ideas about death, falling short of adult understanding in various ways. Teenagers, though, are able to understand death as well as adults—intellectually, at least—and teenagers also think about death quite a bit.

What Teenagers Think

In her book *The Anatomy of Bereavement* Beverly Raphael cites a study that was conducted on 1,421 teenagers in a death education program in Melbourne, Australia in 1979. According to researchers D. Tobin and D. Treloar, about 43 percent of the teens in this program said that death was upsetting because they feared it might be painful. Some 41 percent were disturbed at the idea of causing grief to friends and relatives, while 29 percent were upset about not knowing what comes after death. Some 26 percent of the teens surveyed said that they disliked the idea of death because it would cheat them out of the life they hadn't yet been able to live and enjoy.

When asked what death meant, some 35 percent of the students said if brought new life after death. About 37 percent described death as an endless sleep or peace, while 22 percent said it was simply the end, our final experience. About 23 percent of the students surveyed said they didn't know what death meant.

The researchers also asked what kind of death the students wanted, if they were able to choose. Some 39 percent said they wanted their deaths to be quiet and dignified, while 33 percent said they'd choose a sudden death, as long as it wasn't violent. About 18 percent of the students wanted to die after completing a great achievement, while 15 percent said there was no kind of death that they would choose.

Finally, the researchers asked students how old they wanted to be when they died. Some 31 percent choose ages 70 to 80; 29 percent chose 80 to 90; and 23 percent chose 90 to 100.

How Teenagers Die

The three most common causes of death for teenagers are accidents, homicide (murder), and suicide, in that order, according to George Howe Colt's 1991 book *The Enigma of Suicide*. Colt points out that although the mortality rate—the percentage of deaths within a given population—has gone down for every other age group in the past 30 years, it has been going up for teenagers. This is largely because of the increase in teenage suicide, but it also may be because of the increased level of violence that many teenagers now confront.

For example, according to figures cited by Scholastic's *Safe Schools, Safe Streets* Teacher's Guide, the risk of dying from a firearm injury has increased 77 percent for teenagers aged 15 to 19 since 1985. Firearm injuries are causing more deaths among U.S. teenagers than all natural diseases combined, and one out of every four people who die of a firearm injury is between the ages of 15 and 24. In other words, according to the National Center for Health Statistics and the FBI Uniform Crime report, 14 teens and children are killed every day in murders, gun accidents, and suicides.

The August 1994 edition of the *Utne Reader* reported similar statistics: In the past decade, the risk of being shot to death for teenagers aged 15 to 19 more than doubled.

In 1990, 3,398 young people aged 10 to 19 were murdered, while 2,237 killed themselves. In the 1980s, 19,346 teens were murdered, while 18,365 killed themselves, making a total of 37,711 teenagers killed by violence—at the hands of themselves or others—during the decade. Today's teenagers run twice the risk of dying by such violence than their counterparts during the most turbulent years of the 1960s.

Students themselves report that they face a shockingly high degree of violence. In a 1993 Harris Poll, some 11 percent of the high school students surveyed said they had been shot at, while 33 percent of the students said they believed they would be shot to death before they reached old age. These figures were corroborated by a 1992 survey conducted by the University of Michigan, which found that 16 percent of the eighth graders, 14 percent of the tenth graders, and 12 percent of the seniors in the poll feared for their own safety.

Even as teenagers fear death at the hands of another, they are becoming more likely to kill themselves. Although people between the ages of 15 and 24 have the lowest suicide rate of any adult age group (while some younger children do commit suicide, their rates are even lower), teenage suicide has increased drastically in recent years, tripling over the last four decades. The real increase might be even greater because some suicides who do not leave notes are recorded as victims of "accidents." And risky behavior—driving unsafely, abusing drugs or alcohol, engaging in potentially dangerous sexual behavior, participating in foolhardy contests or challenges—may lead to death, suggesting that the "foolhardy" teenager may be acting out of a sense of despair and also, perhaps, from a wish to die.

Even teenagers who wish passionately to live must confront the possibility that their sexual activity could threaten them with death. Some 50,000 teenagers aged 15 to 19 suffer from syphilis, a potentially fatal STD (sexually transmitted disease). The fastest-growing group of people with AIDS (Acquired Immune Deficiency

Syndrome)—another fatal STD—is teenagers. According to the Centers for Disease Control, the incidence of AIDS among 13- to 19-year-olds increased by 61 percent between February 1988 and 1989 alone, while according to the August 3, 1992 issue of *Newsweek* magazine, the cumulative number of 13- to 24-year-olds diagnosed with AIDS increased 77 percent between 1989 and 1992. Since the epidemic began, more than 5,000 children and young adults have died of AIDS, making it the sixth leading cause of death among 15- to 24-year-olds, according to the same issue of *Newsweek*.

Although the popular myth about AIDS suggests that only gay men are likely to get it, that is not at all true, particularly among teenagers. Heterosexual contact has generated about 6 percent of all AIDS cases in the general population, but among 13- to 24-year-olds, heterosexual contact has caused 12 percent of all AIDS cases. Overall, AIDS strikes nine times as many men as women—but for 13- to 24-year-olds, the ratio is only four to one. This suggests that teenagers are taking enormous sexual risks, primarily having sex—heterosexual *or* homosexual—without a condom, and/or engaging in anal sex, which is generally considered the greatest risk, even with a condom. (See *Straight Talk About Sexually Transmitted Diseases* by Michael Brodman, M.D., John Thacker, and Rachel Kranz. Also see Chapter 7 for hot lines and resources that can help you find out more about safe sex.)

Thus, teenagers today live in a world where they feel threatened by violence, where they witness an increasing number of teenage suicides, and where they know that engaging in a sexual relationship might threaten their lives or the lives of those they love. Teenagers also witness death on a larger scale, reading about wars in various parts of the globe, seeing wars on TV, having friends or relatives serve in the armed forces, and knowing that one day they too may be drafted or decide to enlist in the military.

Teenagers may be aware of many other types of death on a large scale. The Los Angeles riots of 1992 brought death close to home for many teenagers. So did the terrorist attack on the World Trade Center in New York City. Teenagers who are concerned about racism, the environment, and the proliferation of nuclear weapons also may see the prospect of wide-scale death threatening their families, their communities, and their planet itself.

In such an uncertain world, how is it possible to cherish life, both your own and that of others? How is it even possible to live life confidently, planning for life rather than death as you grow into adulthood?

These are complicated questions. Before we consider them, let's look first at the particular challenges of teenage life and at how teenagers in other cultures cope with the ever-present reality of death.

Death in the Midst of Life

The teenage years are a very special and difficult time. On the one hand, you're just finding out how much you can do—what you're now capable of that you couldn't do before. On the other hand, you're also coming up against your limits. When you were little, you may have thought of yourself as smart, or good at sports, or maybe possessing a special talent, such as sports or music. Now that you're older, however, you're getting a more realistic sense of what it means to be good at things—how much there is to know, what it takes to be a real athlete, how a really good musician sounds. Just as you're starting to be able to do more, what you can do may seem like less.

In other parts of your life, too, you're getting more freedom and responsibility—but you probably want still more! If you're allowed to go out alone at night with your friends, you may be questioning why you still have a curfew. If your parents are letting you date, you may resent their rule that they have to meet and approve of your potential date before you're actually allowed to go out. Just as the world of adult rights and responsibilities is opening up to you, it also seems to be closing off, as you realize how much further you have to go before you're really as free and as powerful as a grown-up.

Another important part of the teenage years is figuring out who you are. Maybe when you were a kid you were good in school, but now that you're older, you might be questioning what you're learning and why. Perhaps when you were younger, your parents offered you music lessons and you accepted without thinking about it too much; now you may be wondering whether *you're* the one who likes the clarinet or whether it's more to your parents' taste.

When you were younger, you probably didn't even think much about *who* you were—you just were. Now you wonder what *your* opinions and tastes are, what *you* think about politics, religion, school, dating, sex, and drugs; what kind of music, movies, and books *you* like; what kind of future *you* want for yourself. You're probably thinking about the kind of person you are too—are you someone who is slow to react to an insult or quick to anger? Do you have one interest that you stick to for a long time, or do you switch quickly from activity to activity? When you were younger, you may have accepted who you were more easily; now it seems as if everything needs to be questioned.

You also may feel that your teenage years are a time of rapid and confusing changes. Maybe when you were younger, you knew you were a certain type of person ("Oh, Theo's the hothead in the family!" "One thing about Janie, she's always liked to keep her room neat." "Give Ed a bat and ball, and he'll have a game organized in five minutes."). Now, though, you may find that you're changing so fast that you don't even *know* how you are—one day you're calm and serene, the next day jumpy and agitated, the day after that fierce and determined. One day you love playing baseball, the next day you feel clumsy and awkward, and the day after that you think it really is a stupid game.

These rapid changes and confusing questions are exactly what the teenage years are for. The passage from childhood to adulthood has never been easy, and these years are marked by intense challenges and, often, intense frustration in all cultures and societies.

In more traditional societies, however, the teenage years are a time of rituals that give a kind of structure to these passages. Interestingly, these ceremonies might be said to mimic the effects of death. These cultures seem to believe that, for teenagers truly to grow up, they must pass through a deathlike time of isolation. Then, having confronted death, the teenager can truly pass into adulthood.

In some cultures, young male teenagers are subjected to heroic ordeals—left to wander through a wilderness by themselves, put in a place where there are believed to be ghosts, or sent to a sacred place where they are supposed to receive visions. In other cultures, female teenagers are secluded in small huts with no windows or wrapped into a hammock so that they can't move. In both cases, when the teenager emerges from the ordeal, it's as if he or she has died and come back to life.

As Robert Jay Lifton explains in *The Broken Connection: On Death and the Continuity of Life,* these ceremonies mimic the psychological experience of being a teenager. In a sense, a teenager "dies" as a child and "comes back to life" as an adult, passing through a challenging ordeal in which he or she often feels terribly alone. As teenagers give up the comforting role of being a child who is taken care of, they need a new vision of who they are, a new way of relating to the physical world, to their communities, and to their own bodies.

In our culture, there are no specific signs or rituals by which a teenager can mark his or her passage into adulthood. Of course, there are some signs that show a person is getting older: Being allowed to date, to drive, and to hold a job are all markers of increased age and responsibility. Going to middle school and high school may seem to mark a passage from the "baby days" at elementary school. Some families celebrate Bar Mitzvahs, Bat Mitzvahs, or Confirmations as a sign that a child has become an adult, at least in the eyes of the religion. For the most part, though, teenagers are left on their own to figure out how childhood dies and adulthood takes its place.

Therefore, the teenage years may be a time when just the *idea* of death seems particularly upsetting or disturbing. Of course, no one really likes to think about death, or to imagine himself or herself as able to die—children, teenagers, and adults all have a hard time with that one! When you're a child, though, you tend not to think about death unless you lose someone, and then you're mainly concerned with how the loss affects you. And for many adults, death may seem easier to face because they know they're living the life they've chosen. They're able to put their energy into shaping their lives, while accepting—at least to some extent—that someday their lives will end.

Teenagers, though, are much more aware of themselves than children are, and yet, unlike adults, they usually don't have the power to make most of their choices in their lives for themselves. Unlike children, they're moving out into the world, testing their power—at school, with friends, maybe on a job, perhaps in athletic competitions or community theater or in a citywide political campaign. Unlike adults, though, they're not in the world on their own—their parents and teachers still make many decisions for them. So they're able to understand death in a way that children cannot, but they're not yet able to accept it the way that some adults can.

After all, how can you accept your death if you feel you haven't even had your life yet? Teenagers are still figuring out what they want their life to be, still just testing out the extent of their powers into the world. At such an age, accepting the reality of death may seem like giving up the game before you've even started!

Coping with Death in the Midst of Life

There are lots of ways to handle this paradox. As we've seen, traditional cultures handle it by giving teenagers huge challenges to face, challenges that require all their energies and talents just to stay alive. How do teenagers in our culture deal with the possibility of death? Here are some ways we've thought of. Can you think of others?

- Ignore it, just don't think about it.
- Listen to sad songs about people dying.
- Get interested in ghosts, ghost stories, and other examples of the life after death.
- Become religious and put faith in a religion's explanation of life after death, such as the Christian idea of heaven, the Hindu idea of reincarnation or the Buddhist idea of Nirvana.
- Write poems, songs, and stories about death and dying.
- Become very frightened of things that used to not seem very scary, such as thinking you hear dangerous noises in the house or worrying about food poisoning.
- Take foolhardy chances by driving dangerously, abusing drugs or alcohol, engaging in risky sexual behavior, and the like.
- Feel depressed, despairing, helpless, and hopeless about life.
- Think frequently about suicide.
- Become preoccupied with someone else's death, whether the death of a friend or relative, a classmate, or a famous person such as a rock star or sports figure.

All of these are natural responses to fears about death—fears that both adults and teenagers share. Of course, not all of these responses are equally safe and healthy! Some of the activities on the list actually may endanger a teenager's life, making death an even greater possibility than it was before. Some of the activities may make a person feel locked into sadness about death, with no chance of getting out into the world and enjoying life. (If you, or anyone you know, is seriously considering suicide, you should get help right away. See Chapter 6 for more information, as well as the hot line and resource numbers in Chapter 7. Likewise, if you or someone you know is engaging in risky behavior, you might want to look at those chapters for ideas on getting help.)

We'd like to suggest two other ways to come to terms with death—ways that may not be as common as those on that list, but which may also be extremely useful.

- **Break the isolation.** As we've already seen, in our culture. the process of death and dying is extremely isolated. But it doesn't have to be that way. Get to know sick or elderly people—relatives, neighbors, or people in your community. Perhaps you're old enough to volunteer in a hospital or nursing home, helping people to write letters, reading or doing errands for people who need help. Maybe your Scout troop, religious group, or school organization can organize something for lots of people your age. Meeting people who are facing death can be an enriching experience, helping you to see for yourself that death is a part of life.
- **Create a support network.** Just because our society tends to value individualism doesn't mean you have to go along with it! As the old saying goes, a problem shared is a problem halved. If you can find ways of talking about death—the losses you've experienced, the fears you have—you can benefit from others' insight, suggestions, and support. Just knowing that other people feel the way

you do may be helpful. Just putting your fears and sorrows into words can make you feel better. Perhaps your school or religious organization can help you start a support group for people concerned with this issue, or maybe you can talk openly and honestly with friends, relatives, or trusted adults. As we've seen, other societies have elaborate networks to help people face death, both in the form of particular losses and in the form of an abstract idea. Reach out and create your own network of support. This may be particularly important if you live in a community marked by violence, a community in which death is *not* isolated but is rather a frequent and frightening occurrence. Finding ways to talk about your feelings—and figuring out ways to fight back—can make you feel better and perhaps can solve at least part of the problem.

3

Coping with Dying

When her mother first started staying home, Felicia was frightened. She didn't know what to expect, and since her father told her not to worry her mother, she was afraid to ask her mother any questions. Even though she tried to avoid her mother as much as possible, her father gave her the job of bringing in her mother's breakfast every morning and taking in her dinner every night.

At first, Felicia didn't even like to stay in the same room with her mother. She would leave the tray and then later come back to pick it up. But for a while, her mother seemed very cheerful. Even though she's always in bed, she doesn't really act sick.

One day Felicia just can't stand it any more and she asks her mother what's wrong.

"Oh, nothing serious," her mother says. "I'm just a little knocked out, that's all. But I know I can beat this thing if I just don't give in to it. Don't worry, Felicia, I'll be fine soon."

Felicia is so relieved she can hardly stand it. "You mean you're not going to die?" she asks.

"Not if I can help it!" her mother says cheerfully, as if it's a joke, and Felicia feels as if a big weight has just been lifted off her shoulders. She starts sitting with her mother while she eats, chatting with her about her day in school and reminiscing with her about things they used to do together. She feels so good that her mother seems all right again.

Then one day when Felicia brings in the breakfast tray, she feels as if she can't do anything right. Her mother is mad because the eggs are cold and the toast is too crisp. When Felicia, trying to be nice, goes to heat up the eggs and make more toast, her mother complains about being left alone. Then when Felicia comes back, her mother says the eggs are too well done and the toast seems raw. "I can't believe I haven't done a better job teaching you to cook!" her mother snaps. "Sick as I am, I bet I could do a better job myself!" Felicia feels very hurt, but her mother really does seem sick, so she doesn't want to argue.

The next week when Felicia comes in, her mother asks her to bring her writing paper and her address book. "Do you really think I should?" Felicia asks. "I mean, aren't you supposed to be resting or something?"

"I just feel so bad about all the friends I've let slide over the years," her mother says. "I know I'd feel better if I could just make that right." Felicia watches her mother, who seems quite weak, struggle to write letter after letter. She doesn't understand why this is so important to her mother.

Then, over the next few weeks, Felicia notices another change. Her mother just lies there, ignoring everything. She doesn't want to talk to Felicia, and when Felicia asks if she can get her mother anything, she's terrified to notice that there are tears in her mother's eyes. She's never seen her mother cry! Something really must be wrong. Felicia starts once again to wonder if her mother might be dying.

Felicia feels so bad. She wishes she could do som
to make her mother feel better. But she can't thi
anything she can do. And now that she thinks her m̲.̲.̲.̲.̲.̲
is dying, she really wants to do the right thing.

Harry never really thinks about it, but somehow, deep
down, he's been assuming that his sad feelings about Clem
will be over within a few weeks—maybe, at most a month.
But here it is, two months later, and he still feels terrible.
Many nights he'll find himself thinking of Clem and crying.
Often, when he's doing something he used to do with Clem,
or when something happens that he'd like to share, he
thinks, "I wish Clem were here." Generally he just feels as
if it's not worth the bother to do anything, because nothing
is going to be any fun anyway.

His parents have noticed that Harry has been having a
hard time, but they don't know what to do about it. A couple
of weeks after Clem's death, Harry's mother suggests that
Harry pick a couple of friends and she'll take everybody to
Action Park for the day. At first, Harry doesn't want to do
it, but she insists, thinking that it will cheer her son up.
Finally, Harry gives in, and they go, but he doesn't really
have a very good time.

A month or so after Clem's death, Harry's father arranges
to go camping with Harry for the weekend. That was
something that Harry really used to love, especially because
it meant he got special time alone with his father. Now,
however, he tells his father he doesn't want to go, saying
that he has too much schoolwork to go away for a whole
weekend. When his father, who is really worried, says that
he'll write a note to the school, Harry insists that he just
wants to stay home. It's almost as if he doesn't want to be
alone with his father.

Then Harry's parents get a call from Harry's homeroom
teacher. She says that all of Harry's teachers are worried
about him. His schoolwork is falling off, he's not paying
attention in class, he's dropped out of the Science Club,

and in gym class, he barely seems to have any energy. "He used to be so good at sports," the teacher says, "but now he's picked last for every team—he just isn't making any effort. And he used to seem to have lots of friends. But now he eats lunch alone almost every day. Is something wrong at home?"

When Harry's mother hangs up the phone, she turns to Harry's father. "I think maybe Harry is still upset about Clem's death," she says. "Obviously we didn't take this seriously enough. But what do we do now?"

After that first day back at school, Carmen doesn't think about Josh any more. After all, she barely knew him. She's busy with schoolwork, with helping Miriam plan her birthday party, and with band practice, where she plays the clarinet. Plus there's a cool guy, Roberto, whom she really likes, and Miriam told her that she heard through the grapevine that Roberto is planning to ask her out. Carmen is really excited, and she and her friends spend a lot of time talking about exactly what Miriam heard and what it might mean. Carmen feels as if she has a lot to look forward to.

But for some reason she starts having a lot of trouble sleeping. Some nights she's fine, but other nights she feels anxious and jumpy. She finds herself feeling very afraid of the noises in the house at night, imagining that a burglar or a crazy person has broken in and is coming to kill her family. If she hears a creak or a bump in her sister's room, she worries that it's the murderer in there, and that nobody else notices because they're all already dead. Carmen knows this is silly, but when the fear comes over her, she really believes she's in danger, and she gets so scared she can't even move.

Sometimes, even when she doesn't get frightened as she's falling asleep, she finds herself getting scared by something that happens in her sleep, either a bad dream or a noise that wakes her up. She'll wake up at 5 in the morning and won't be able to get back to sleep again.

Carmen doesn't want to tell anybody else about her night fears and her sleeping troubles. She's kind of ashamed of being such a baby. But one day Miriam says, "Carmen, you look terrible. Come on, what's wrong?" Carmen finds herself telling Miriam all about it.

"You should see a counselor," Miriam says emphatically. "You should see a counselor right now. Girl, Roberto is thinking about asking you out! You want to look fresh, not all worn and tired." Miriam takes Carmen by the arm and pratically drags her to the counselor's office. "Now you tell that man the truth, the whole truth, and nothing but the truth," Miriam tells Carmen before she goes in. "How else is he going to help you?"

Carmen actually is pretty scared about seeing the counselor. But she also thinks, "Maybe he really can help." If someone really could tell her how to sleep peacefully again, it would be such a relief!

When a Loved One Is Dying

One of the most useful of all human abilities is the capacity for *empathy*—the ability to feel what another person is feeling. Usually we develop empathy because we have shared an experience that another person is going through. When we see a friend's team lose a game, we can say "I know how you feel" and mean it if we have ever played on a losing team. When our brother's girlfriend breaks up with him, we can say "You must be feeling awful right now," and the tone of our voice can let him know that we too have felt the pain of rejection and the pangs of unrequited love.

But how do we feel empathy for someone who is going through something that we have never experienced? One of the most painful parts of watching a loved one die is knowing that he or she is really alone with the experience. We haven't "been there" too; we can only imagine it.

One of the most helpful approaches to caring for a loved one who is dying has come from the psychiatrist Dr. Elisabeth Kübler-Ross, who for many years studied and cared for terminally ill patients. Through her extensive study, Kübler-Ross identified five stages, which she believes affect virtually every dying person: *denial and isolation, anger, bargaining, depression,* and *acceptance.*

These five stages have been the subject of a great deal of misunderstanding. Some people took Kübler-Ross's theory to mean that every dying person goes through every single stage in the same order. Other people assumed that if a dying person did *not* pass through each stage, he or she did not have "a good death"—that he or she had not fully come to terms with all the emotions that dying brings up. Still other people assumed that these stages applied not only to the person who was dying but also to the people that loved him or her.

We believe that Kübler-Ross's stage theory is very useful—up to a point. We think that many dying people *do* experience some or all of the stages she identifies, and that being aware of these stages may help the rest of us understand what a terminally ill person is going through.

However, as you read about each stage in the sections that follow, it's important to keep in mind that these stages don't necessarily happen in a particular order or even one at a time. As John S. Stephenson stated in *Death, Grief, and Mourning: Individual and Social Realities,* rather than thinking of people passing through separate stages, it's more helpful to think of a person's emotions as a "hive of [feelings], in which there is a constant coming and going." Stephenson was quoting psychologist Edwin Shneidman, who says further that people who know they are dying experience many different and contradictory emotions at the same time: "disbelief and hope . . . anguish, terror, acquiescence and surrender, rage and envy, disinterest and ennui, pretense, taunting and daring and even yearning for death," all in the context of "bewilderment and pain."

Stephenson also points out that some psychologists have noticed anxiety as a major emotion in dying people, because they fear the unknown realm into which they are passing. He cites other researchers who found that some patients either withdrew or committed themselves to an energetic life—and then simply continued that pattern until they finally died. Clearly, even the experts don't agree on how people die.

Even though not every terminally ill person will necessarily experience all of Kübler-Ross's stages of dying, we think it's helpful to be familiar with each stage as she described it. While we can't know from our own experience what a dying person is going through, understanding Kübler-Ross's stages can help us to use our imaginations to grasp what the dying person might be feeling.

We also might begin to understand the limits of our empathy. Sometimes, if a person really is alone with an experience, it's not possible to say "I know how you feel." But it may be possible to say, in words or with actions, "I hear what you're saying—and I'm here for you." Understanding Kübler-Ross's stages of dying might help us better understand what a dying person is going through, so that we can be there for that person in a loving and supportive way.

Denial and Isolation

According to Kübler-Ross, a person's first reaction to being told he or she is dying is simply not to believe it. In fact, that is almost everyone's reaction to dying. After all, every one of us, without exception, is going to die someday. But how many of us believe it? Although we may be able to imagine getting hurt, what we can't imagine is simply ceasing to be, no longer being a living person with thoughts and feelings and the ability to affect the lives of others.

Perhaps this *denial* has its uses. It may be that in order to mobilize our energy for living, the human psyche simply refuses to accept the possibility of death. Yet when a person is terminally ill, death shifts from a possible future into a very real presence. Death is no longer something that happens "someday" or "to other people." Death is something that will happen to us, and soon.

Most people can't make an immediate transition from their usual state of denial into a full awareness of their approaching death. So, as on one level their minds are getting used to the idea, on another level they are refusing to accept it. They might say, "I'm not really going to die—this is just a minor illness." Or perhaps, "I don't think this doctor knows what she's doing—I'd better get a second opinion." A person might imagine that someone mixed up the test results or switched the X rays. He or she may say "I know I can beat this thing," or "None of these doctors knows what they're talking about." Felicia's mother seems to have been in this stage when she told Felicia, "I know I can beat this thing if I just don't give in to it."

Another form that denial may take is refusing to care for oneself properly. A heart patient, for example, may insist on exertion that doctors have cautioned against. A person on a special diet may blithely continue to eat regular food, even if that causes pain and threatens further medical complications. People in denial may hope desperately that if they act as if everything were fine, it will be. They may worry that if they acknowledge that there is a problem—my heart can't take this activity; my liver can't tolerate that food—then they will somehow make the problem "real."

Families and friends also may practice denial. In fact, according to Kübler-Ross, people who are dying frequently have an easier time accepting death's approach than those who love them. The dying person's denial may be an effort to play along with loved ones, hoping to spare them pain or fearing that they will abandon the dying person if his or her insistence on the truth becomes too unpleasant. People who are dying may sense who is comfortable with their condition and who is not and try to go along with whatever a loved one or a hospital visitor needs to believe.

However, most people need some time to get used to the idea that they have a fatal illness. Whether they continue to hope for recovery or not, eventually they must accept the reality of their situation—but this awareness may take time.

While they are still in the denial phase, dying people may protect their denial through *isolation*—separating themselves from those they love. They may separate themselves through busyness, or spending so much time searching for new doctors, new treatments, or new healing techniques (such as faith healers or psychics) that they have no time to spend with others. They may withdraw emotionally, spending more time alone or refusing to see hospital visitors. Or they may withdraw more subtly, talking and passing the time with those they love but refusing to talk on any deep emotional level. All of these kinds of isolation serve the same purpose—to keep the dying person from recognizing the reality of his or her situation until he or she is ready to deal with it.

During this phase, Kübler-Ross suggests that friends and family just stay cool. After all, it isn't up to them to say when another person "should" be ready to face a difficult and unpleasant reality. They may stand firm on issues of actual health care, refusing to cooperate with someone who ignores a diet, avoids taking medication, or otherwise disobeys "doctor's orders." But this is quite different from insisting that a person discuss what is about to happen.

Eventually, says Kübler-Ross, a dying person may be ready to talk about his or her feelings about the reality of death. Usually this happens late at night or in the early hours of the morning, when we all feel most alone—and so, perhaps, closer to death. If loved ones have conveyed the message that they are there for the dying person, whenever he or she is ready to talk, they then can have the satisfaction of being of real help, ready to listen and be supportive whenever the person begins to break out of denial.

Anger

Once a person has accepted that he or she is going to die, the next thought is usually "Why me?" Realizing that something bad is going to happen often makes people very angry. So once a person has accepted that he or she really is dying, all sorts of things that normally would seem trivial or even pleasant suddenly become infuriating.

Felicia's mother's complaints about breakfast are one example of this kind of anger. As you can see, a lot of the anger comes from frustration. It's hard for Felicia's mother to accept that she's not well enough to get up and fix her own breakfast, that she has to depend on Felicia to do it for her. At another time, she might even enjoy being cared for by her daughter—but this time, she has to face that her daughter's care *means* that she herself is dying. When her mother is feeling especially angry about dying, all of Felicia's efforts to be helpful seem like just one more painful reminder that she'll never fix breakfast again and that she won't be around to teach Felicia to cook—or anything else.

This kind of anger also may include *envy.* People who realize that they are dying may, for a while, feel unable to bear the sight of those who have a longer time to live. "How dare you go on living while I have to die?" a person might think at this stage. "How come you get to enjoy your children while I have to leave mine? How come you get to go on and have a future while mine ends here? Why do you get to walk around in a healthy body, able to leave this room whenever you like, while I have to lie here in bed, and I can never get away from the most important fact in *my* life—that pretty soon I'm going to die?"

Like Felicia's mother, a person in the anger stage of dying often will find fault with everything around them. A hospital visitor has come too late, too early, or on the wrong day.

A get-well present is the wrong size or of no use. Like Felicia, a child bringing food to a parent might find that nothing tastes good or is properly cooked. A dying person might convey that he or she doesn't want visitors or that they can do nothing right.

Another part of this angry reaction is anger at the universe, at life in general, even anger at God. "Why me, God?" the dying person may think. "Why are You punishing *me* like this? Haven't I been a good person? I hate You for doing this to me!" If the dying person's loved ones are religious people, this anger at God can be particularly hard to take, especially if they are turning to their God for faith and solace during this difficult time.

Clearly, a dying person's anger is a very hard response to handle. Felicia, for example, was focused on trying to make her mother feel better. It hurt her a great deal when her mother suggested that all of her efforts were worth nothing. It also made her mad. After all, it wasn't her fault that her mother was dying! And what about her own feelings? Maybe her mother was losing her life, but she, Felicia, was losing her mother! Then Felicia felt guilty for being so selfish, and depressed that she only seemed to be able to make her mother feel worse, not better.

How can loved ones handle the anger of a dying person? First, it may help just to know that anger is almost always part of the experience of dying. It's no reflection on the dying person's friends or family—it doesn't necessarily mean that the dying person had a bad life, was badly treated before, or is being badly treated now. (Of course, it *might* mean that there is a concrete problem that needs to be solved. That's why anger is such a difficult reaction for hospital personnel to deal with. Often it's hard to tell whether the person's anger is a general reaction to death or a specific reaction to bad treatment—or perhaps both!) Knowing that a dying person is likely to be angry, though, may help keep loved ones from taking that anger personally.

It also may help to realize that the anger is a kind of blessing in disguise. Sometimes anger actually can help dying people to recover or at least to live longer, as they battle for the life they believe they have a right to. After all, why do we get angry? Often because we believe that something isn't fair, that we have been cheated out of our rights. A dying person who believes that he or she has the right to stay alive may be more likely to live longer than a person who passively accepts the inevitability of death.

The anger is also a sign of how much the dying person loves life and therefore how painful it is to let go of it. If Felicia's mother didn't care about her daughter, it wouldn't be painful to imagine a time when she could no longer teach her how to cook. If she didn't care so much about her family, it wouldn't be so painful to imagine leaving them all.

If loved ones understand where the dying person's anger really is coming from, they also may be able to imagine how hard it would be to watch others enjoy what you must give up. They can allow the dying person to ask the question "Why me?" without expecting to answer it. Perhaps that way they can help the dying person move through the anger as it arises.

Bargaining

One response that many people eventually have to the idea of their death is bargaining—what Elisabeth Kübler-Ross calls coming to a "temporary truce." In effect, the dying person says, "All right, I accept that I have to die—but not yet! Just let me do this one last thing—*then* I'll be ready to die!" Or the bargain may extend over a longer period of time: "If I become a truly good person, can I live for another 20 or 30 years?" A religious person might think, "If I start practicing my religion regularly, God, will You grant me a long and healthy life?" Someone else might think, "I've always regretted having that fight with Maude. I see now it was all my fault. If I apologize to her, can I get well again?"

Some people believe that the impulse to bargain while dying grows out of guilt. They point out that we all have things in life that we regret doing or not having done. Realizing that we're going to die soon makes us aware that we'll never get another chance to atone for our mistakes. The dying person's bargaining may be partly a way to try to wipe out the guilt before he or she dies. Thus, Felicia's mother feels guilty about losing touch with friends and takes steps to get back in touch. This is both a responsible way of responding to a genuine regret and a kind of bargain with death: "At least let me live until I've finished writing these letters!"

Friends and family of a dying person may or may not be aware of the bargaining that is going on. Dying people themselves may not see their reaction that way. Yet if loved ones are aware of this possible reaction, it may help them to understand the intensity that a dying person might bring to a project, a request, or an idea. To the dying person, the idea may have come to stand for his or her very hope of survival.

Depression

In many ways, depression is the most common experience of terminally ill people, and probably it is the hardest for loved ones to deal with. Depression, according to Kübler-Ross, sets in when the dying person realizes that he or she really is going to die. No new doctor, no rage against the hospital, no bargain with the universe is going to change that. Other specialists have noted that this reaction may occur as soon as the person gets the news of impending death and may last until the person actually dies. Even in that case, though, depression is likely to be interspersed with other reactions and emotions as well.

It might be helpful to think of a dying person's depression as a kind of work. After all, dying people are getting ready to say good-bye to their whole lives. In a way, they're leaving their past, their present, and their future. As they draw nearer to death, they realize that, to some extent, their memories and their past experiences will die with them. No one knows for sure whether a dying person can carry these memories and experiences beyond the grave, so the dying person is facing the loss of everything that has made his or her life meaningful and worth living.

The dying person also is saying good-bye to the present—to all the people he or she knows, to all the activities he or she enjoys, to the daily experiences of eating a delicious meal, seeing a sunset, or hearing a beautiful piece of music. Perhaps the dying person's illness has already taken away many of life's pleasures. He or she needs time to mourn these losses and to say good-bye.

And the dying person also is saying good-bye to the future. Dying people are confronted with the fact that, if they have children, they won't live to see them grow up. They can imagine their husbands, wives, or friends going on into the future, meeting new people and having new experiences. Perhaps they've been looking forward to a child's graduation, to a special vacation, to new projects at work, or to retirement. Now they must face the fact that death has cheated them out of the future they thought they could count on.

You might think that a person who is facing such terrible losses would be feeling very sad. In fact, often such enormous sadness is too much to bear, especially at first. Instead of feeling sad, it may be easier to feel angry. And if a person is afraid to be angry, or is tired of being so, he or she may become *depressed*.

Depression often is confused with sadness, but the two feelings are really very different. In fact, depression is often a kind of numb state, a lack of feeling. Or it may be a feeling of being hopeless and helpless, so that feeling sad doesn't even seem worth while, because life is so awful.

True sadness—mourning, grief—may be cleansing and healing, but depression brings no relief. It just seems to go on and on. A dying person who is depressed is in effect saying "I don't want to feel sad about my death and all the things I'm losing. I'm so angry that I can't stay alive! If life is so unfair as to bring me death, then I just won't feel anything! I won't feel anything and I won't do anything, I'll just lie here and suffer."

Of course, depressed people usually aren't conscious that this is what is going on inside. They may not realize that when they are ready to feel their sadness, they can find a new kind of acceptance and peace, and face death. They may not be able to handle such enormous waves of sorrow, or they may fear that their families, friends, and neighbors "need them to be strong." Certainly, if a person has been depressed often throughout life, he or she is likely to become depressed when facing death as well.

As we've seen, this reaction is particularly painful to people like Felicia, who want to reach out and comfort the dying person, to share their last days or weeks together, to feel part of the dying person's life as long as possible. Depression, though, has the effect of shutting everyone else out, as if the depressed person were saying "You can't do anything to help me, so why don't you just go away?" When people are depressed, they simply may not be able to receive comfort or help from another, or they may feel safer keeping people at a distance. They also may feel over-whelmed with their own sadness about dying, and may be unable to realize that their loved ones are also sad.

Perhaps the only thing that a loved one can do in the face of a dying person's depression is to accept whatever feelings the dying person has, without trying to fix things or cheer the person up. Acknowledging and accepting the person's feelings and situation may be helpful—"Yes, it's true, you probably won't live to see another spring. It must be so hard to say good-bye." "I see how hard it is for you to see your grandchildren. I'm sorry it's so hard." "You must really miss Aunt Louise. I'm sorry she can't be here with you now."

Of course, people whose loved ones are dying have feelings of their own to deal with. They won't always be able to respond to the dying person's needs—there will be times when they have to take care of themselves, too. (For more on taking care of yourself, see below.) But as a general rule, if you can allow depressed people to feel whatever they are feeling, you may be giving them the greatest gift of all—the space to go through their final days with the support and acceptance of the people who love them.

Acceptance

Acceptance, which Kübler-Ross calls the last stage of dying, has caused perhaps the most controversy of all her stages. According to Kübler-Ross, the dying person who has been allowed to work through all of the other stages finally will arrive at acceptance—the recognition that death comes to us all and that it can somehow be accepted as the natural end to life. Rather than submitting in bitter defeat, Kübler-Ross says, a person can find peace and serenity, even a kind of victory, in accepting the reality of death while making the most of life. In fact, she says, this kind of acceptance is a goal that we can all strive for, since we all must die someday.

Many other psychologists, however, believe that true acceptance of one's own death really is not possible. They claim that people who are terminally ill become depressed and remain depressed until they die. To these psychologists, it seems unfair or even cruel to expect that a dying person would somehow "accept" his or her death.

Perhaps there is no real resolution to this controversy. Whether a person arrives at—or even desires—an acceptance of death may be more a matter of individual personality and philosophy than a principle of what "dying people in general" go through.

If we look at literature, we certainly find both types of attitudes represented, particularly as people have written about the deaths of their loved ones. The poet Dylan

Thomas, for example, did not expect or even want his aged father to find "acceptance" as he died. He wrote:

> Do not go gentle into that good night.
> Old age should burn and rave at close of day;
> Rage, rage, against the dying of the light.

On the other hand, when the philosopher William James was facing *his* elderly father's death, he wrote his father the following letter, expressing both his own acceptance and his hope that his father too could accept the inevitable end:

> We have been so long accustomed to the hypothesis of your being taken away from us, especially during the past ten months, that the thought that this may be your last illness conveys no very sudden shock. You are old enough, you've given your message to the world in many ways and will not be forgotten . . . And it comes strangely over me in bidding you goodbye how it is so much like the act of bidding an ordinary good night. Good night, my sacred old Father! If I don't see you again—Farewell! a blessed farewell!
>
> Your William

Taking Care of Yourself

One of the hardest tasks for people who are caring for the sick and dying is to remember to take care of *themselves*. It may seem that the dying person should always take precedence, that his or her feelings are the most important, that what he or she wants should be done if at all possible. It also may seem that it's unfair, selfish, or cruel to say "No," to take a break, to have a good time, or to think about yourself.

Felicia has trouble with this. She finds herself looking at herself in the mirror when she brushes her hair in the morning, thinking "I'm so selfish. Here I am worrying about whether I look good, and my mother is dying!" Or she'll be eating lunch with friends at school and find herself laughing hard at a joke someone tells. Right in the middle of her laughter, she'll think, "How can I laugh at a time like this?"

Here are some feelings that may come up in people whose loved ones are dying:

- **Guilt:** "How can I go on living and enjoying myself when my mother is losing her life?"
- **Envy:** "How come Sarah gets to have both her parents, and I have to watch my father die?"
- **Fear:** "What's going to happen to *me* when Mom dies?"
- **Anxiety:** "What if there's something I could be doing that I'm not doing?"
- **Anger:** "It's not fair! Children are supposed to have both parents and all their brothers and sisters! I shouldn't have to go through this!"
- **Resentment:** "Billy's really being a pain this week. I don't care if he's dying—he's driving me crazy!"
- **Frustration:** "I've tried and tried to cheer Grandpa up, but nothing I do seems to work!"
- **Loneliness:** "It seems like my parents have been thinking about Jenny for months. I can't even get them to pay attention to me long enough to sign my report card."
- **Shame:** "I must be really selfish—Nana called me and I kept her waiting for half an hour while I fixed myself a snack."
- **Embarrassment:** "I don't know anybody else who has someone dying in their family. I don't like being different."

Is it helpful to hear that all of these feelings are normal? Everyone, no matter what age, goes through some if not all of them when facing a loved one's illness or dying. It's probably even harder for teenagers to go through these feelings, because of the special age they're at. Children probably don't expect themselves to help out as much as teenagers do, and grown-ups expect less of them. Grown-ups, on the other hand, have been alive longer and have been through more. They may have a more realistic idea of how much they can do for someone else, and they also may know themselves better. They may have learned by now that just because they think of themselves occasionally, that doesn't make them selfish people; that just because they sometimes make a mistake, that doesn't make them bad people.

It may be that family members and friends need to make special efforts and sacrifices when someone they love is ill. And if you're in that situation, you'll have to do some hard thinking about what you do and don't want to do to help out. Whatever you decide, though, remember that we all need to take care of ourselves, that we must feel free to enjoy our lives even while someone we love is losing his or hers.

Here are some things you can do to take care of yourself if someone you love is dying. If a friend or relative is going through this situation, you might want to share these ideas with him or her.

- **Take care of your health.** Be sure you get enough nourishing food and sleep, and exercise as well. Not only will this make you feel better, it will give you more physical and emotional energy to help take care of your loved one too. It certainly doesn't make things easier on anybody if you also get sick!
- **Find someone to talk to.** If it's a family member who's dying, and you can talk about your feelings with other family members, that's ideal. Together, you can share memories, frustrations, sadness, anger, and, perhaps, acceptance. Ideally, you can have time to spend alone with the dying person, time to spend together as a family, and time to spend with family members who are not dying.

  Sometimes, though, that just isn't possible. And even if it is, it may not be enough. Figure out which of your friends can lend a sympathetic ear, and *talk away*. Help your friend understand that you don't need him or her to "solve your problem," you just need someone to listen and maybe to cry with. If you also can talk to other adults whom you trust, that's even better. But don't try to go through this alone—people just aren't made that way.

You also might want to get help from a counselor or therapist. For more on how to get help of all kinds, see Chapters 6 and 7.

- **Give yourself some time off.** Everybody needs a break. Figure out the kinds of breaks that will help you to "get away from it all," and take them! Maybe you're the type who relaxes in a long, hot soak in the tub. Buy yourself some bubble bath and let that private time be your special treat. Or maybe your idea of a perfect day is going to the mall with the gang and stopping for pizza on the way home. It might not be possible to do this as often as before your loved one got sick, but make sure you do it at least once every couple of weeks! Some people find it soothing to take a walk in the woods or the park. Others escape by watching funny movies or reading spy stories. Figure out a bunch of different "escapes" that will work for you, and get yourself away at least once every couple of days or so. Your emotions are already working overtime; they need some time off.

- **Stay in touch with your feelings.** The person you love is going through a lot right now—but you are too! Maybe you'll find it helpful to write about it in a journal, to draw pictures about it, or just to spend some time thinking in a quiet place. Realize that you're likely to feel many different feelings, some warm and loving toward the dying person, some angry and resentful, some fearful and anxious. The more willing you are to feel these different emotions, the more easily you'll pass through them. (Again, if particular feelings are giving you trouble, you may want to see a counselor. See Chapters 6 and 7.)

Feeling and Letting Go

Did you know that people grieve and mourn not only after a loved one dies but also before? If a person really understands that a loved one is dying, he or she can take these last days, weeks, or months to feel sad—but also to make the most of the time that is left.

Sometimes this is hard to do. Just knowing that someone is going to leave may make it hard to enjoy their company while he or she is still around. You may have noticed this as friends prepare to leave town on the last day of school, or when you're saying good-bye to a friend who's moving away. You're so prepared for the sadness you know you'll feel that you just want to hurry up and get it over with. You think maybe that way, it won't hurt so much.

If you can let yourself feel sad, and if you can share this sadness with the person who is dying and with other people, you may find that something else happens too. You also get in touch with all of your love for the person who is dying, with all of the memories you share and with the ways that he or she will always be a part of your life. That's why it's so important to spend time with the person you love, remembering things together, talking about your feelings, or just sitting quietly in each other's company.

Some people find it hard to open up and do this when someone they love is dying. They're so afraid of feeling sad about the person's death that they can't stand to think about him or her at all. What these people find later, however, is that they didn't really save themselves any sadness. They just put their sadness off for a later time—after the person has been dead for a while. What they *did* miss is not the sadness but their last chance to share their love.

If someone you love is very sick, it may be difficult to spend time with him or her in the ways that you're used to. And the person may be going through his or her own version of defending against sadness—the dying person may not want to see anyone he or she loves, because it will seem too sad. This may be hard for you to accept, and there may not be anything you can do about it.

Even if the two of you can't share them, though, *you* can still hold on to all of your good feelings and memories about the person who is dying. You can make yourself a scrapbook of things you did together, go for a walk to places you used to visit, write in your journal about things you've shared, or draw pictures to remind yourself of happier times. You can allow yourself to feel all your love for this person, to feel all the ways that he or she has been special to you, to think about all the ways that he or she will always be important to you. In fact, only by letting yourself have all your feelings about the person who's dying will you be able to let that person go when the time comes.

When a loved one dies suddenly, there is no time or opportunity for grieving before the death. Sudden death may leave us feeling that there is "unfinished business," such as having had no chance to say good-bye. This means that the grief work must start after the death. That will be the time for resolving the "unfinished business" by, for example, expressing feelings, writing in a journal, being with others who have shared the loss, reliving happy experiences and memories of the person who has died with them, and eventually, after feelings have had a chance to be expressed, letting go of the grief.

4

Coping with
Death

Felicia is getting more and more worried about her mother. She knows that her mother is terribly sick and she's pretty sure her mother is dying, but no one will tell her anything that is going on. Her father already has told her not to talk about it with anyone, and she feels so alone.

Then one day Felicia's mother calls her daughter over when Felicia is bringing in her dinner tray. Although Felicia knows that her mother is very weak and in a lot of pain, her mother tries to smile. "Listen, Felicia," her mother says, "I'm so sorry, but I don't think I'm going to get any better."

At first Felicia is really frightened. She doesn't think she should be hearing this. "Do you want me to go get Dad?" She asks. "Or do you want your pills or something? Maybe I should call the doctor. You're going to be all right, Mom, really, you are."

"No, Felicia," her mother says firmly. "Really, I'm not. The doctor thinks I've only got a couple of weeks left. I don't want to spend them pretending. I want to spend them being with you, and your father, and your brothers."

Felicia is so shocked, she starts to cry. She's cried alone in her room before because she's been so scared and so upset, but this is the first time since her mother got sick that she's cried in front of her. Her mother holds out her arms, and Felicia goes and puts her head on her mother's chest. Her mother holds her for a long time until she stops crying.

After that, Felicia and her mother spend a lot of time together. They talk about the things they've done to-gether—shopping trips to the mall, the family vacation last year to the Rocky Mountains, the day Felicia had the starring part in the school play and her whole family came to see her. Her mother tells Felicia about things that she remem-bers about *her* mother, from when *she* was a little girl. Felicia talks to her mother about what subjects she likes in school, and what things she likes to do besides study, and what she thinks she'll do when she grows up.

Sometimes these times together are almost happy, as they remember something funny that happened or talk about good times that might happen in the future. Sometimes talking about the memories and plans makes Felicia sad, as she thinks about the time when her mother won't be there any more. Sometimes it hurts Felicia to see her mother getting weaker and looking worse and worse, and some-times the two of them just cry together.

One day Felicia gets home from school and her mother is gone. Her father has left a note saying that she's at the hospital. He asks Felicia to take care of her younger brothers and to be brave—he says he'll call as soon as there's any news. Felicia doesn't understand why she and her brothers can't be at the hospital too. After all, she's their mother. If she is going to die, her children should be with her. But all she and her brothers can do is wait for the call.

Finally, late that night, Felicia's father calls her from the hospital. It's all over. Her mother is dead.

One day Harry's parents have a special appointment to go to. They won't tell Harry what it is, but when they come back, they call Harry over and sit down for a talk.

"We went to talk to our rabbi," Harry's mother explains, "because we've been worried about you and we didn't know what to do. And he thought maybe part of the problem was that you never really got a chance to feel sad about Clem's death. Everybody was concerned about his family, but you were his friend—you loved him too. Nobody thought about what *you* needed."

"Yeah, well, it's too late now," says Harry. "Anyway, that was a long time ago. I don't even think about it anymore."

"Maybe you don't," Harry's father says. "But I know when my mother died, I was really sad about it for at least six months, and I thought about her a lot for a year or more. I know it was really important to me to go to her funeral, and to sit *shiva* for her, and to go to the unveiling of her headstone a year later. And even now, every year, I light a *yahrzeit* candle to her memory, because even though I'm still sad she died, it makes me feel better to remember her."

"But it's too late for me to go to Clem's funeral," Harry says, "even if I wanted to go, which I didn't."

Harry's parents look at each other. "The rabbi suggested that you might want to have some other kind of ceremony to remember Clem," Harry's father says. "Maybe with some of Clem's other friends."

"I know you were his best friend," Harry's mother says, "but I bet other people miss him too. I think maybe you'd feel better if you got together and remembered him together."

"How would that help?" Harry asks angrily. "It would just make us all feel worse!"

"Why don't you think about it?" Harry's mother suggests. "Think about a ceremony or something special you could do to remember Clem."

At first, even thinking about the talk with his parents makes Harry mad. Why are they bringing this up now, just as he's getting over Clem? Where were they when he died? How come then they told him that he was "just a friend," and now they're saying he's important?

Then Harry starts thinking about what they said. He knows that Jamal and Eddie were also Clem's friends. When Clem died, none of them even talked to each other. In fact, he hasn't seen either of them since Clem died, except in school. Maybe it's because none of them want to be reminded of Clem. Maybe there is something they could do.

Harry knows that in his religion, they don't believe in people living somewhere else after they die. But they do believe in people living in each other's memories. So if he and his friends can all remember Clem, it will be like keeping him alive a little longer.

When Carmen goes to see the counselor, a funny thing happens. She starts out talking about Josh. But as she talks longer, she finds herself remembering her grandfather.

Carmen's grandfather died when she was only eight years old. She barely knew him—but she remembers him very clearly. "He always wanted me to give him a big kiss hello and good-bye," she remembers. "But he held me real tight, which was really uncomfortable, and he always smelled funny. Sometimes he would get mad and yell at mom, and she would always be down and depressed after we visited him. Nothing could cheer her up."

When Carmen's grandfather died, everyone agreed she was too young to go to the funeral. Her father did take her aside and explain that "Mommy is very sad because Grandpa was her daddy that died." Carmen felt bad that her mom felt bad, but she also was secretly glad that Grandpa had died. Now there would be no more weird visits that made her uncomfortable and made her mom feel sad.

At the same time, the eight-year-old Carmen felt kind of guilty to feel glad. Look at how bad her mom felt—why didn't Carmen feel just as bad? Also, Carmen really wondered about that funeral that she wasn't allowed to go to. She wondered what Grandpa's body looked like after he died, and what they would do with the body. When she told her friends that Grandpa had died, one of them told her that they put the body into the ground, where it rots, just like a mushy old banana, and worms crawl in and out of the eyeholes while they eat the eyes. This was so gross that it almost made Carmen throw up.

The counselor helps Carmen understand that part of why Josh's death is freaking her out so much is because her feelings about him are getting all mixed up with her feelings about her grandfather. A lot of her trouble sleeping goes back to things that scared her and made her feel guilty when she was eight years old. After a while, those eight-year-old feelings seemed to go away—but they didn't really go away. They just "went underground," and now that someone else has died, they're coming back again.

Carmen also realizes that she genuinely does feel bad about Josh. She can imagine how lonely he must have felt, because sometimes she feels lonely too. But those real feelings that she has now are getting confused with feelings that came from a death that happened when she was little. The feelings belong to a time when nobody tried to help her understand what death meant or what really happened to a dead body.

The Necessity of Grief and Mourning

Perhaps the most awful thing about the death of a loved one is that nothing prepares you for it. Even if you have already lost someone you loved, a new loss is just as sharp and painful.

Some people have a hard time dealing with the enormous grief that losing a loved one brings on. They may feel—about their own grief or that of others—that feeling bad is a kind of disorder or weakness. We don't look at it that way. We—along with virtually all psychologists and experts who study grief and mourning—consider mourning a necessity. In fact, if people don't go through a period of processing their feelings—*especially* if the person who died is someone they had mixed feelings about—their feelings are probably being buried, and they may explode later. Thus, Carmen had a lot of feelings over her grandfather's death—grief, fear, sadness for her mother, worry about what happens to dead bodies, relief, resentment, and curiosity. Because there was no place for her to experience these feelings when she had them, they came out later as fears about Josh's suicide.

Alternately, if a person avoids grief, other parts of his or her life may be affected. Thus, Harry's grief over Clem's death came out as depression—he just didn't feel like doing anything, his schoolwork suffered, and he didn't want to make any more friends. In order to get back his pleasure in the rest of his life, he's going to have to find a way to feel sad about Clem first, so that he can mourn his friend and let him go.

In her book *About Dying: An Open Family Book for Parents and Children Together,* Sara Bonnett Stein says:

> Mourning is not just feeling sad. It is the specific psychological process by which human beings become able to give up some of the feelings they have invested in a person who no longer exists, and extend their love to the living. Mourning is hard, emotional work. It is pulling memories into focus, and allowing ourselves to be touched by the feelings they carry with them. It is struggling with guilt that we might have done better and anger that we are left alone. It is taking up the disrupted threads of our life and finding new patterns to weave of them. It is giving up a person who is no more.

One way to look at the mourning process is to divide it into stages. Of course, everyone's experience is different. But in our observations, most people go through three stages: *chaos, expression,* and *understanding.* These stages can take months or even years to go through. They don't proceed in a straight, unbroken line—a person might be in stage 1 for a week, move on to stage 2, and then have days of feeling like he or she is back in stage 1 again. But if a person continues with the work of grief and mourning, sooner or later he or she will move on.

The First Stage: Chaos

Right after a person has lost a loved one, he or she may feel overwhelmed by all the feelings that come flooding in. If you are in this situation, you may first feel numb, dazed, in shock, or strangely calm. You may be sure that it is all a bad dream or a misunderstanding of some kind. You may feel very frightened, vulnerable, or unsafe. Or you may feel caught up in the throes of a pain so intense that you can't think clearly and can only hurt.

One common reaction at this time, especially among teenagers, is *denial.* Denial is your emotions refusing to accept that something bad has happened. Although you have been told that a loved one has died, your emotions don't respond in a way that fits that news. Instead, if you're in denial, you feel calm, detached, perhaps even cheerful. (You may have noticed this reaction in yourself at other times of stress: hearing that a surprise exam is being scheduled for tomorrow, listening to a boyfriend or girlfriend break up with you, or staring at the letter that tells you that you didn't get into the college you wanted to.)

Actually, denial is a fairly healthy way to respond to bad news. It allows your body, mind, and emotions time to mobilize their resources to cope with the problem. If you have to take action, such as care for younger brothers and sisters or help clean the house for the funeral reception, denial helps you put your feelings "on hold" while the necessary work gets done. You might think of denial like the brake on a car that's going 60 miles an hour, headed for a bump in the road. If the car hit the bump at top speed, the consequences would be much more serious than if the car hit the bump at 15 miles an hour. Denial works like that, softening the blow by making some space between your hearing of bad news and your reaction to it.

Teenagers often respond to this Chaos stage by a kind of pulling in. It's as if their whole systems just shut down in self-defense. It's very common for teenagers facing a death simply to withdraw and refuse to talk about their feelings or to spend time with family and friends. In a way, this reaction is like looking for a safe place to hide, a search for protection against this new source of pain.

This first stage may last any amount of time. For some people, it extends through the funeral and the reception afterward, if there is one. Then, when the body has been buried or cremated and all the guests have gone home, reality sets in, leading them to stage 2.

Other people move through the chaos stage much more quickly. Still others move through it more slowly, feeling numb, in denial, or "on automatic pilot" for weeks. If a person is in this stage for too long, refusing to talk about the death or to deal with his or her feelings more directly, he or she may need help in moving on. (See Chapters 6 and 7 for more on getting help.)

The Second Stage: Expression

Sooner or later, most people do move on. The denial and numbness wear off and their protection is lost (although these responses may return periodically for weeks, months, or even years, along with other responses). As reality creeps in, all sorts of feelings emerge and people respond in many ways. Here are some feelings and responses that we ourselves have felt or observed.*

---

*We are indebted to Earl A. Grollman, author of *Straight Talk About Death for Teenagers: How to Cope with Losing Someone You Love,* for his concise and complete summary of reactions.

COPING WITH DEATH 73

- **Embarrassment:** "Everyone will know this about me. And I'll be the only one without a mother—I hate being different!"
- **Abandoned:** "Nobody loves me, nobody understands me, everybody has left me all alone."
- **Anger:** "Why did this have to happen to me anyway? And my friends are no help—they say nothing, or else they say the wrong thing, which is worse. I hate those doctors—why couldn't they save my daddy's life? And most of all, I hate my father—how could he leave me like this?"
- **Envy:** "Why does everybody else have two parents and a happy life?"
- **Panic:** "How will I ever make it through the day? Who's going to braid my hair now that Mom is gone? What if Dad can't take care of us by himself—will we have to move in with somebody else? What if he gets married again? Will things ever be normal again?"
- **Relief:** "It was so awful to watch her get sicker and sicker—I'm glad that's over with," or "I didn't like my grandpa anyway, it's kind of a relief that he's gone," or "I loved my grandmother, but when she was alive, we weren't allowed to make any noise and Mom and Dad were always sad. Maybe now things can get back to normal."
- **Loneliness:** "Clem was my best friend and he really understood me. Nobody else will every understand me the way he did. Besides, they're all busy this weekend. Clem would have had time for me."
- **Guilt:** "How can I be alive while he is dead? It isn't right!"
- **Regret:** "There were so many things I should have told Clem. And I shouldn't have made fun of him when he struck out that time. I wish I could turn back the clock—I'd do so many things differently!"
- **Yearning:** "Wouldn't it be great if she were here with me now? I'd tell her everything, and she would under-

stand. I *wish* she were here. I *wish* she were here right now!"

- **Depression:** "I feel so miserable. I know I'll never be happy again."
- **Feeling sick:** Some people have trouble sleeping. Others get headaches, stomachaches, or nausea. Still others have trouble breathing, think they're choking, or feel dizzy. Sometimes a person surviving a loss gets very tired, almost as if he or she were trying out what death might be like.
- **Feeling crazy:** Some people think they see the dead person walking ahead of them on the street or in a crowd. Some people find themselves getting lost in places they know well, or making stupid mistakes without realizing it until afterward. Some people find themselves talking to the person they lost, or speaking of him or her in the present tense, or dreaming intensely about him or her, or calling the person on the phone. Some people think they hear voices or footsteps, or they hear someone calling their name.

Coping with Stage 2

How can people handle the intense feelings that come up during this stage? Of course, there are no easy answers. Coping with grief *is* painful, no matter what you do. But, as Doug Manning, author of *Don't Take My Grief Away*, puts it, you don't have to feel bad *about* feeling bad! You can accept that it's natural and right to feel intense pain—*and* to feel anger, envy, relief, and all the other feelings that might seem "bad" or "wrong." You can try to accept the fact that *no* feelings are "bad" or "wrong"—they're just how you feel.

You also can accept that sometimes you may *not* feel intense pain. Sometimes you may find yourself laughing at a joke, or enjoying a tender moment with a boyfriend or girlfriend, or excitedly making plans to spend the day with a best friend. You may find that some things can still give you pleasure even in the midst of pain.

Sometimes people feel guilty for feeling good after something bad has happened. They may feel as if it's not fair that someone they love has died and they are still alive. Or they may feel that if someone they love has died, their own lives should stop too, as if they *had* died, as if the death had the power to stop both the life of the person who died and the life of the person who is left behind.

These kinds of feelings are known as *survivor's guilt*. Survivor's guilt is especially painful if the mourner had any kind of mixed feelings about the person who died. If the person who died was someone who abused the mourner, or gave him or her a hard time, or whom he or she sometimes loved and sometimes hated, or whom he or she sometimes loved and sometimes didn't even think about, the mourner may feel especially guilty. The mourner may feel that if he or she had had a better relationship with the person who died, the person would still be alive.

Of course, logically speaking, that feeling doesn't make any sense. People don't die because of how we feel about them. Our thoughts and feelings don't have the power to kill another human being. It would be nice if our love and our willpower could keep other people alive, but unfortunately, human beings don't have that godlike power. But even if we understand this rationally, deep down, our feelings may *wish* so hard that we had this power that we come to believe that we really do—and then we feel guilty when we "fail."

How can people cope with this mix of feelings and thoughts, logic and irrationality? Here are some suggestions that have worked for us and the people we know. Maybe you, your friends, and your family can think of others.

- **Give yourself some time off.** Think of grief and mourning as a job you have to do. It's hard work to feel all the different types of feelings that come up after the death of someone you love. But you can't do any kind of a job 24 hours a day. You'll "work" better if you have some time off from your grief.

Time off might come in many different forms: a walk in the woods or by the lake; going to a funny or a thrilling movie; getting deeply involved in a school or community activity, such as theater, music, sports, or a neighborhood recycling project; taking a trip to visit a friend or relative out of town. You need to make sure your mind, your body, and your emotions don't get *over*worked, so that they are in shape to *do* their work.

Finding ways to let yourself laugh—at a funny movie, fooling around with friends, telling jokes and funny stories with family members about the person who died—may be a wonderful way to take care of yourself. Laughter actually can help people recover from diseases; it's one of the human body's "natural medicines." Some people feel guilty about laughing during a time of grief and mourning, but we think of such occasions as a gift. As Earl A. Grollman said in *Straight Talk about Death for Teenagers,* "Cry when you must; laugh when you can."

- **Talk about your feelings.** Sometimes you'll need to take some time off, but sometimes you'll need to do your "grief work"—and you'll find that you can do some of it better with others. Find someone—preferably several people—who are willing to sit with you and let you talk, remember, yell, wonder, and cry.

  The people who are best to talk to are the ones who aren't frightened by strong feelings. (Many people in our society are!) They may have lost a loved one themselves, so they can say truth fully, "I know how you feel." Or they simply may love you and want to be there for you. The best listeners at a time like this are people who *can* listen, people who will accept whatever you need to say, without needing to correct you, fix things for you, or make the pain go away. Find the people who can hear you say "Sometimes I loved my father a lot, but sometimes I just couldn't stand him!" or "You know, when my sister died, I was actually relieved. I was so tired of her getting all the attention all the time, just because she was sick." People who are good to talk to might include friends, religious leaders, a school counselor, a sympathetic teacher or family friend, or relatives such as aunts, uncles, and cousins.

- **Stay in touch with your family.** Sometimes when teenagers lose a loved one, their reaction is to pull farther away from their families, especially if the person they loved was someone within their family. It's as if they're trying to protect themselves from further hurt by not getting close to anyone else. Sometimes too, other family members are struggling with their own grief, so that they are the ones who pull away or seem hard to reach.

  If you're in that situation, find ways to connect to the family members who are left. You actually may need to "make a date" to talk: "Can we spend some time together today after school? I just need to talk about Dad for a while."

  Two kinds of family time are important: one on one, and together as a family. In *Don't Take My Grief Away*, Doug Manning describes how, when his wife's father died, he and she pulled away from each other, failing to talk about what the death meant to each of them until a great deal of time had passed. Each was afraid to share his or her feelings with the other. Although he and his wife finally did talk, they never spoke about the death with the other adult children, the wife's brothers and sisters.

  Manning realized that the family had lost a very precious opportunity to share memories and feelings. Now, as a minister, he makes sure to organize a special "family time" for immediate family members to be alone with each other—without friends or extended family—for at least an hour or two before the funeral. He says that this family time is especially important if anyone had mixed feelings about the person who died. The family time is a chance to share feelings and memories, to realize that you are not alone with your grief, even though you also are alone with it.

As a teenager, it may be hard for you to help organize this kind of "family time" for your family. But if the idea makes sense to you, give it a try. You may find a religious leader, another relative, or another immediate family member who thinks this is a good idea too and can help make it happen.

- **Spend some time alone with your thoughts, feelings, and memories.** An important part of the work of mourning is processing your thoughts, feelings, and memories about the person whom you've lost. To quote a line from Robert Anderson's play *I Never Sang for My Father,* "Death ends a life, but it doesn't end a relationship." Part of the work of mourning is to change the relationship, acknowledging the lost person's importance to you, saying good-bye to what is really lost, and discovering what parts of the relationship you will always keep. In a way, this is a lifelong process, but you can begin it in this stage of mourning.

  We suggest keeping a journal in which you feel free to write your private thoughts and memories. Some people find it helpful to write letters to the person who is gone. Others like to make lists, "What I miss," "What I don't miss," "Things I remember," "Why I'm angry," "Why I'm sad," and so on. Still other people like to draw pictures, or make collages, or find other visual ways of expressing their feelings.

  We strongly suggest that you find some way of expressing yourself, however, rather than just sitting and thinking. Often, in grief, your thoughts can chase themselves around and around in a circle. Expressing them, getting them "outside yourself" by writing about them (or, at other times, by talking about them), can help you move to a new place with them, finding new realms of sadness and anger, and also, eventually, new realms of comfort and acceptance.

- **Take care of yourself.** Sometimes "survivor's guilt" can lead a survivor to neglect himself or herself—to avoid eating, sleeping, or getting fresh air; to have a hard time bathing, grooming, or keeping clothes in order; to let a bedroom get really messy and disorganized; to be careless physically or to get cut, bruised, or scratched in a lot of little accidents; or even to take big physical risks, such as walking alone in a dangerous neighborhood or driving while drunk or high. It's almost as if the survivor is saying "I have no right to be healthy and happy; I have no right to enjoy my body or my life. I don't deserve to enjoy the pleasures of being alive."

  Taking care of your body and your space may be especially difficult after a death, but we urge you to do it. Eating healthful food, getting enough sleep, and getting some form of exercise several times a week will help your emotional state as well as your body. Taking care of the space that you live in will help you feel that *you* are worth taking care of. You deserve care, love, and attention—keep on giving them to yourself! After all, as we've said, grief and mourning are hard work. You need to keep in shape for them.

- **Take care of yourself sexually.** Another way that people sometimes don't take care of themselves after a death is sexually. Sometimes, after a loved one dies, people turn to some form of sexual contact for comfort—hugging, kissing, making out, or intercourse itself. Physical closeness can be a good thing. Being held by someone who cares about you or taking pleasure in your body and its ability to make you feel good are ways of being comforted and feeling "alive," especially after you've confronted someone else's death.

  On the other hand, in our society sex is often a very difficult area, especially for teenagers. Sometimes sexual relationships can be caring and loving, but sometimes they can be one-sided, punishing, or abusive. If you get involved when you're feeling grief, you may end up only feeling worse. If you get involved because you need to feel loved, but your partner is not interested in that kind of emotional relationship, you also might feel abandoned twice—first by the person who died, and second by the person who "didn't love you enough." If you're the one who just needs physical contact while your partner is looking for an emotional relationship, you might end up hurting other people without meaning to. And of course, if you don't practice "safe sex," you may be risking pregnancy, disease, and even death. (For more about "safe sex,"* see *Straight Talk About Sexually Transmitted Diseases,* by Michael Broadman, M.D., John Tacker, and Rachel Kranz, or call one of the hot lines listed in Chapter 7.)

After a loved one dies, your judgment and your feelings will naturally be shaky. Find ways to get the love and comfort you need without hurting others, or yourself, and without exposing yourself to needless risks.

- **Be especially careful with drugs and alcohol.** When you're feeling pain, sometimes all you want is to make the pain go away. You may feel tempted to turn to drugs or alcohol at a time like this, hoping to blot out the pain, to help yourself sleep, or to give yourself a good time. You may even feel that you have support for this reaction—after all, don't many doctors prescribe tranquilizers and sedatives to help their patients cope with pain and stress? What's wrong with trying to "medicate" yourself?

  Although some doctors prescribe sedatives and tranquilizers for grieving patients, no prescription drug can solve or cure grief. Prescribed drugs might help a grieving person get through the first day or so, but over an

---

*There are many things you can do to make sex safer, but in fact no sex is completely safe.

extended period of time, we believe that tranquilizers and sedatives actually interfere with the mourning process. The problem with legal and illegal drugs, as well as with alcohol, is that although they temporarily mask or numb your feelings, they actually make your period of grief last longer.

The sad but true reality is that the hurt feelings will go away only after an amount of time. Nobody can say what that amount is or should be for you—you'll know it only as you live it. But you won't lessen your pain by masking it with drugs, you'll only put off feeling better.

Alcohol and marijuana are both depressants, as are tranquilizers and sleeping pills. That means that they slow a person's system down, and they can often make people feel sad and depressed as well, either while under the influence or after the drug has worn off. Likewise, with "uppers"—cocaine, amphetamines, and other stimulants—the high is always followed by a crash. Even if you feel better while you're up, you're guaranteed to feel a lot worse while you're down.

Experimenting with drugs and alcohol is a risky business at any time. When you've lost a loved one, the risks from drugs and alcohol are much larger, both to your overall health and to your long-term recovery from grief. If there is any one time to be careful with drugs and alcohol, it is after losing a loved one.

- **Ask for help when you need it.** In our individualistic society, it's easy to feel that we should be able to handle everything by ourselves. We look at our cultural symbol of the lone cowboy riding into the sunset or the action hero taking on thousands of bad guys singlehanded, and the idea of crying, feeling confused, or asking for help seems like an unforgivable weakness.

  In fact, it takes great strength to know what you need and ask for it. The help you need may be available from your friends, family, religious community, school, or neighborhood. Or you may need another kind of help—counseling, therapy, a support group. *Everyone* who goes through a serious loss needs help of some kind—there are *no* exceptions to this rule! Be sure that *you* are getting the kind of help that you need. (For more on getting and finding help, see Chapters 6 and 7.)

Specific Concerns

A death brings a profound emotional upheaval among family, friends, and community. It also raises some practical questions and concerns. Here are some issues that teenagers who survive a loss are often faced with, along with our suggestions for dealing with them.

- **Do I go to the funeral?** This has got to be an individual decision. And in some cases, the final decision may not be up to you. Your family may have strong feelings about this issue. If the person who died is a friend, that person's family may have the last word.

  In general, we believe that it's important for children and teenagers to be permitted to attend funerals, memorial services, and other occasions to commemorate a death. For teens as well as for adults, such public ceremonies are valuable ways of dealing with a difficult time. They help to make it seem real that the person has died, allowing mourners to move on with their grief. They help to make it clear that the person's life mattered in the world and that he or she still has living and loving friends and relatives who will keep the person's memory alive. This can be a comforting feeling even in the midst of a very sad time.

  If you feel strongly that you would like to attend a funeral, within your own family or someone else's, start by expressing this wish to whomever is in charge. If that doesn't work, try to find a supportive adult who can speak for you—a religious leader, an adult relative, a family friend, a neighbor, a teacher, even your school counselor.

Likewise, if you feel strongly that you *don't* want to attend a funeral or wake, make your feelings known and, if necessary, enlist the help of an adult who also can speak on your behalf. Before you make this decision, however, you might think about where it's coming from. Is it that you're afraid or unwilling to see a dead body? You can easily attend a service without doing so; in fact, many services are "closed casket," so that no one can see the body. Is it that you're not yet ready to accept that the person is really dead? Sadly, not going to the funeral won't bring the person back to life—and it may make it more difficult for you to move on through your grief.

If you're confused about this issue, we strongly urge you to talk with someone you trust in time to make your decision. It's easy to think that there will always be time to make a decision or to change one's mind. Funerals—and death itself—are sad reminders that this is not always true.

- **A friend or distant relative has died; or a friend's family member has died. What do I say to the other people who were close to that person?** Helpful things to say are things that acknowledge the person's pain without trying to take it away or make it less. For example, you might say:

"I'm so sorry this happened. I'm here if you ever need to talk."

"What can I do to help?"

"Let me know if I can help."

"One thing I'll always remember about [the person who died] is . . . "

"You're not alone. I'm here when you want me."

"Talk. I'm here to listen."

"[The person who died] meant so much to me. I'll miss him/her too."

"Go ahead and cry. I'm here."

What usually isn't helpful is to guess at the person's feelings, to tell the person what to do, or to explain why the person doesn't need to feel bad. Things that are usually *not* helpful to say include:

"I know just how you feel."

"You'll get over this sooner or later."

"You must feel terrible."

"Don't take it so hard."

"Just think happy thoughts."

"Remember that this is God's will."

"[He/She] was suffering so much—this is for the best."

If you have gone through a similar loss, you might mention your experience, briefly, without comparing:

"I lost my mom last year. I know it's hard."

"When I was 10, my best friend was in an accident too. I'm here if you ever want to talk."

- **One of my parents has died. What's going to happen to me now?** One of the hardest parts about facing a parent's death as a teenager is having not only your emotional world turned upside down but also the day-to-day events of your life. There may well be changes that you're not happy with—having to move, taking on more work at home, giving up some after-school activities. You may have some say in these changes—or you may not. That's the hard part of not yet being an adult.

    We suggest two ways of coping with this situation. One, encourage the adults who are responsible for you to share with you what's going on. Convey that you are ready to hear about the problems that they are facing and that you would like to help solve them if you can. Or if you would rather *not* know about any decision until it is final, communicate that. Just as you have never before been in this situation, neither have they. Letting them know what you want, what will work best for you, and how much involvement feels right may make things easier all around.

    Two, be aware that no matter what decisions are made,

they will not affect you forever. When you're 18, if you don't like conditions at home, you can go off and make a home of your own. If your family has to move to a smaller apartment or another city for financial reasons, you may discover some good things about the change. But even if you don't, sooner or later you *will* be able to choose where and how you want to live. Do your best to accept patiently what you can't change, and concentrate on what you can change.

The Weeks and Months after the Death

This is in some ways the hardest period of all. The immediate business of dealing with the death is done—you've heard the bad news, the funeral is over, you've gone into and out of shock, you've spent a lot of time crying. Now it's time for life to get "back to normal"—except nothing will ever be normal again. How do you cope?

As with all the other aspects of grief, there are no formulas. But it may be comforting to know that what you are going through is what people *do* go through after a loss. To quote Doug Manning in *Don't Take My Grief Away:*

> If I could do what I wanted to do for you right now, I would make you feel normal. I would hold your hand as you told me of the feelings you are having inside, and I would say—
> Yes, that is how it feels to be in grief.
> Yes, that is a normal reaction.
> Yes, as you progress through grief you have thoughts like that.

Thus, Manning says, a passage through grief can be eased somewhat by knowing what to expect. Here are some landmarks along grief's journey that a teenager who has lost a loved one might encounter.

- **Going back to school.** Some people find a kind of relief in getting back to a normal routine—and some also find themselves feeling guilty at this relief ("How can I *enjoy* this time not thinking about Clem? I should be thinking about him every minute!"). Other people find that returning to school is especially painful, particularly if the person they lost was someone whom they would have seen at school. Every detail may reminds them of the person they have lost, and it may feel as if they are losing him or her all over again.

Sometimes people find themselves bursting into tears at unexpected times. In the weeks or months after loss, something may remind them of the person they lost, or they may just find tears coming to their eyes without even knowing why. If this is the experience that you or someone you know is having, try to accept those tears may be a sign of strong, deep feeling. Although some people still regard tears as a sign of weakness, we see them as a sign of strength—the natural result of strong love or friendship. (Of course, people who never cry may feel just as strongly. Everyone shows feelings in his or her own way.)

Another difficult part of going back to school may be handling the reactions of people who know about the death. Unfortunately, in our society, many people are very uncomfortable with the topic of death and dying. They may wish to avoid the subject altogether, or they may say stupid or insensitive things. They may try to help you by giving you advice that to you seems foolish. ("Now you can forget all about that." "You'll meet somebody else soon!" "Just try to put it out of your mind.") They may even make jokes about it, simply to handle their own discomfort or anxiety.

If the person who says something unhelpful is not a close friend, you may simply want to say "Thanks for your concern" and change the subject. But if you feel that your friends are also off the mark, try to find a way of sharing your real feelings with them. ("I'm not ready to forget about Clem yet! He was my best friend!"

"Sometimes when I think about Josh's death, I feel lonely too, like maybe nobody would care if *I* died." "I don't really need you to give me advice. But I do need you to listen and understand what's going on with me. Can you do that?")

- **Deciding whom to tell—and how.**   When you go back to school—and to the rest of your life—you may encounter many people who haven't heard about the person's death. Someone may casually ask you, "Oh, how's your sister?" or say, "Give my regards to your mother." If the person who died was a friend, even people who know about his or her death may not realize how much you are affected by it, or they may not be aware that a close friend of yours has died.

   Running into people who aren't aware of the event that has so shaken *your* world can be very upsetting. It may seem like yet another painful reminder of your loved one's death—is it really so easy, then, to disappear without a trace? What does a life mean if a person can die while everyone else's life just goes on?

   Your own feelings about how much to tell people, when to tell people, and whom to tell may change as the weeks and months go on. There may be times when you simply don't have the energy to bring up the subject or to correct the person who refers to "your mom" or "your folks." There may be times when it's important to say "My sister died last year," or "Maybe you haven't heard, but my best friend died last month." You may want to share with people how you feel—"It's still pretty hard for me"—or you may just want to give them the information.

   Sometimes, especially for teenagers, talking about the death of a family member or friend can feel almost embarassing, as if you were sharing something "weird" about yourself. If someone asks, for example, "So what do your parents do?" it would be really awkward to say, "Well, my dad is dead, and my mom is a teacher." If someone asks "How many brothers and sisters do you have?" it may feel strange to say "Two, but one is dead." But simply not mentioning the person who is gone may feel even worse, like a betrayal, or like a way of lying about your own identity. (For more about death and relationships, see Chapter 5.)

There are no easy solutions for these situations. Nor are there solutions that will work all the time. It may help to know, however, that as you work through your own mourning process, this type of situation will get easier for you. Just say what feels right to say, and know that as you become better able to accept your loved one's loss, telling—or not telling—others about it will be less and less of a charged issue.

- **Watching other people's lives move on.** One of the hardest parts of the mourning process is realizing that not everybody goes through it in the same way. If, say, your mother has died and you're still overwhelmed with grief, it may feel like a violation to watch your younger sister come home from school apparently cheerful and happy, laughing with a friend. Or if your best friend was killed in an accident, you may be shocked to see his girlfriend going out with other guys while you're still crying yourself to sleep every night.

  People often have a range of feelings in situations like this. They may feel outraged that life can go on "just as if nothing had happened"—why doesn't this beloved person's death make the whole world stand still? They may feel envious—how come other people seem to be able to move on, while they are still mired in grief? They may feel lonely—now even the other people who loved the lost person are moving on and leaving them. They may feel guilty for wishing that they too could have fun or forget about the death for a while. And they might feel embarrassed, as if their reaction were wrong and the other person's were right.

  In fact, you have no way of knowing what it means when other people apparently are moving on. They may indeed be at a different stage of their grief from you—or they may simply be handling their grief in a different way. They may have felt differently about the lost person than you do, or they may have other ways of showing their feelings. Certainly losing a loved one is a very lonely experience, reminding all of us that we are born alone and we die alone, no matter how many wonderful connections we make along the way. Recognizing that you are also experiencing your grief alone—even if you can *also* sometimes share it with others—may compound those feelings of loneliness and abandonment.

Whatever your reaction to watching others move on—or seem to move on—be assured that this will happen not once but several times as you mourn the person you have lost. You will have both the experience of watching others seeming to be happy and carefree while you're sad and of watching others seem to be grieving while you're temporarily happy. As in all of life's journeys, people move through grief and mourning in different ways and at different speeds. Learning how to accept these differences while staying connected to each other is one of the most difficult—and most reward- ing—parts of growing up.

- **Missing the loved one at special times.** Felicia noticed that, after her mother died, she went through a long period of feeling miserable. Finally, very slowly, she started to feel better. But then her birthday came around. This was going to be Felicia's first birthday without her mother—and suddenly she missed her mom so much she could hardly stand it.

  Harry had a slightly different experience. He was at a baseball game with his dad when suddenly he started feeling sick. At first he thought it was just too many hot dogs and pretzels. Later, though, he realized that he and Clem always used to go to ball games together. Going to his first game without Clem made him feel guilty, as if he were betraying his friend. He felt that if he couldn't go to the games with Clem, he shouldn't go with anyone at all.

People's journeys through grief never follow a straight line. The journey takes twists and turns, particularly when mourners reach a place that they had once visited with the person they've lost. That "place" can also be a holiday or special day, a "first time without so-and-so," or an event that you know the deceased person would really have enjoyed if he or she were still alive.

Sometimes people miss loved ones at turning points or at the beginnings of new adventures. A girl who has lost her mother, for example, might miss her mom intensely on her first date, because suddenly she wishes that her mother were there to share this new experience. A boy going off to camp for the first time might have moments of wishing that a deceased best friend were going with him. Bringing people we've lost along with us throughout our lives is one of the things that our feelings and our memories can do for us. It's a way of keeping the relationship alive, even though the person is not.

Sometimes people don't want to celebrate holidays and special days after they've lost a loved one. Or they may want to create new rituals, finding new ways to share special times that won't seem so much like "something's missing" without the loved one's presence. They might even create new ways of acknowledging the death as part of the celebration, such as reading a Christmas poem that "Jennifer always used to love," or using a dead mother's favorite tablecloth at the Passover Seder.

Deciding how to handle special times without a loved one can be very challenging. As with other aspects of grief, you and your family's ways of handling these events may change as the weeks, months, and years go by. Perhaps you decide to skip the first special time while celebrating the second one just the way you always have. Or perhaps you work as a family to create new rituals, right from the beginning. Thinking about what you want, how you feel, and how you can best express your feelings to others is the best thing you can do for yourself as you move through these special times after a loss.

- **Dealing with the first anniversary of a death.** One of the hardest times after a death is the one-year anniversary. Even if your grief has eased in the past weeks or months, it may come back stronger than ever at this time. Many people find that they feel sad every year on the anniversary of a death, even if they don't feel much grief at other times of the year.

   Some cultures and religions have special ceremonies to acknowledge these anniversaries. In Judaism, for example, children (traditionally, sons) say *Kaddish*, a prayer after death, in memory of a parent. Families also light *yahrzeit* candles—candles that are literally for the *time (zeit)* of *year (yahr)* that a person died. On the first anniversary of a death, there is usually an *unveiling,* a special ceremony to place the person's headstone at his or her grave.

   If your family or religion offers ways to commemorate the anniversary of a death, you may find comfort in those rituals. If your family does not traditionally mark these occasions, and if you find yourself feeling sad at the one-year mark, our advice is to create your own ceremony. Find something that you can do, with family and friends or alone, to acknowledge the death of the person you loved and to mark that person's importance in your life. You might take a walk to the places that you and the person used to go together, write the person a letter, visit the person's grave and speak to him or her, or get together with friends and family and tell stories about what you remember. Know that anniversaries usually are hard for everybody who survives a death, and allow yourself whatever time and space you need to grieve again.

The Third Stage: Understanding

David Crenshaw, in *Bereavement: Counseling the Grieving throughout the Life Cycle*, writes:

> No one ever completely recovers from the loss of someone they deeply loved. Recovery from grief means you can face and bear the loss, but you are permanently changed as a result of the experience. Some of these changes may be positive as we may gain or discover strength within ourselves.

After you've gone through all the stormy feelings, the anger, the pain, the guilt, and the yearning; after you've felt your grief subside and then felt it recur again, stronger than ever; after you've gone through some of the first times and special times without the person who died; then, finally, you start to accept what happened. You start to make some sense of what's left. You start to go on with your life.

It's fashionable in some circles to talk about "resolving" one's grief. We don't believe that grief is ever fully resolved, particularly if one has lost a parent, a sibling, a spouse, or a child. It's not as if you stop thinking about the person or stop missing him or her. It's just that, somehow, you come to understand and accept that, eventually, everybody dies. This makes sense in your life in a way that it couldn't while the grief was still fresh. While you are still grieving, your emotions are saying "*NO.* I'm not yet ready to let that person go." When you move into the stage of understanding, your emotions are saying "*Yes.* That person is gone, and I am here, and I may be sad that he or she is gone, but I am glad that I am here."

Somehow, in stage 2, the loss of the person who died feels very personal. In almost all cases, whatever other feelings are there, the mourner can't help feeling angry at the person for leaving, can't help blaming himself or herself for somehow letting the person go. In stage 3, the survivor comes to accept that the death doesn't *mean* anything about him or her. Even if the person who died deliberately chose death through suicide or through markedly unhealthy ways of living, that choice was his or hers; it was no reflection on the survivor. The fact that the survivor is a person who *can* be left just makes him or her human—we can *all* be left by people who die (or by people who simply reject us). Stage 3 is when the survivor comes to see the death as part of a universal human condition and not something that has been *done to* him or her personally.

We don't believe anyone *can* move into stage 3 without going through stages 1 and 2. If the person who died was very close, it may take the survivor a year or more to move out of stage 2, even if he or she is already very wise, even if he or she has lost someone close before.

As with the other stages, too, the first movement into stage 3 is not necessarily final. A survivor may have moments of deep understanding, feeling that sense of peace and acceptance (along with sadness) that comes at this stage, only to flip back into the missing or longing that he or she felt before. People who lose their husbands or wives are counseled not to marry again before three years, because it takes most adults that long to be sure they really are responding to the new person in their life and not simply seeking a replacement for the wife or husband who died.

We also believe that, at some point, you have to choose stage 3. You can't choose it too soon, or you may not have done all the work of grief and mourning that goes on in stage 2. But if a person doesn't choose stage 3 at some point, he or she could spend a lifetime in stage 2. He or she could organize a whole life around feelings for a person who is gone. Instead of the survivor being at the center of his or her own life, that life becomes a kind of shrine or memorial to the person who died.

What are the signs of moving into stage 3?

- **You're able to think about the bad parts of the person who died as well as the good parts.** You don't need to make that person, or your relationship to him or her, perfect. It's easy, after a person first dies, to remember only the good things about him or her. Somehow it's harder to say "Mom was great, but boy, she lost her temper so fast sometimes!" or "Most of the time Clem was good to talk to, but there were times when he just didn't get the point. And I couldn't talk to him *at all* about music. He just didn't get it." When you feel comfortable remembering the bad with the good, you're on your way to finding a *real* place for the person in your memories and your life.

- **You're able to accept that there will be other people in your life to love.** Of course, every relationship is special. But when a person dies, sometimes our relationship to that person seems to be in a class of its own—*nothing* will ever make us feel as good as that relationship did, and now it's gone. (Something similar happens when we break up with someone we loved, or when a close friendship ends.) Moving into stage 3 means understanding that, special as that person was, there will be other people to love too.

- **You're able to give up or put away the "relics" of the person who died.** When someone first dies, we want to keep them with us as long as possible. Felicia wanted to keep the pots and pans in the kitchen just the way her mother had had them. Harry had a book he had borrowed from Clem that he was supposed to return. He left it out on his dresser as if he had to remember to bring it back to school the next day. These were their ways of holding on to their loved ones as they mourned. Some people find themselves suddenly developing the handwriting of the person they lost, or hearing themselves using the person's pet phrases.

Sooner or later, though, we accept that the person is gone. Felicia and her father rearrange the kitchen to suit themselves. Harry gives Clem's book to the library—he has photographs and presents from Clem to remind himself of his friend. Felicia and Harry won't forget about the people who died, but they won't organize their lives around them either.

- **You're able to accept that you can be happy and that your happiness does not depend on the person who died being here with you.** Of course, you always may be sad when you think of a loved one who died, but you also find that that sadness doesn't keep you from being happy with the loved ones who are here. When you're in stage 2, the person who died sometimes seems to be everywhere. Your grief is like dye, flowing through all the parts of your life and marking them with its special color. When you're in stage 3, your feelings about the person who died is like a room that you sometimes go into and more often stay out of. It's there—but it's only one part of your life.

5

Death
and
Relationships

By the time Felicia hears that her mother is dead, her brothers have already gone to sleep, but Felicia's father tells her not to wake them. He'll wake them himself when he gets home. "You shouldn't have to tell them, Felicia," he says. "I can do that."

Felicia has been expecting this moment for so long, but now that it's come, she just doesn't feel anything. All she can think about is what will happen to her. Who will do all the work her mother used to do? While her mother was sick, a lot of things just didn't get done. The home care worker helped with the cooking, but she won't be coming back any more. Will Felicia have to do all of that? And what about all the questions she's had for her mother? Even though her mother was sick, they could still talk. Will she have to ask her father everything now?

Then Felicia starts to wonder what her father will do. Will he be so sad that he can't handle anything? Will he not want them to talk about their mother dying, the way he didn't want them to talk about her being sick? What if he gets so lonely and depressed that *he* gets sick and dies? Or what if he decides to get married again? Part of Felicia wishes he *would* get married again, right away, so there will be a mother in the house again. Part of her knows that if her father *ever* gets married, *ever,* for the rest of her life, she'll never speak to him *or* his new wife again. How could he treat her mother like that?

Felicia feels silly for worrying this way, and she feels selfish for thinking only about herself. But right now, that's all she can manage.

Harry decides that he does want to have a memorial service for Clem. He invites a couple of Clem's other friends to figure it out with him. They decide that they'll hold the service in the park where they all used to play ball together, and where Harry and Clem used to go for hikes. Everyone will bring something that reminds them of Clem, and if people want to, they can tell stories about things that they remember about him. Harry's parents offer to invite Clem's family to the service, and the boys agree. They also invite their softball coach and Mr. Jensen, Clem's favorite teacher.

Some people come to the service without bringing things, but Harry brings the catcher's mitt that he used to play catch with Clem. His friend Roger brings an issue of Clem's favorite comic book. Courtney brings a video of a movie that she and Clem watched together once. Harry starts the service by saying "We're all here to remember Clem, so if anybody has anything they remember, they can speak when they want to." At first, nobody wants to talk, but then Roger gets things started by remembering a time about four years ago when he and Clem took the bus downtown together for the first time. After Roger breaks the ice, other people share their memories, and pretty soon everyone is talking about Clem. After everyone who wants to speak has had a chance, everybody goes to the refreshment stand and buys a hot dog—Clem's favorite food.

Harry feels both happy and sad to be there. Sometimes, as he listens to the stories, tears come to his eyes. Sometimes he feels that he misses Clem so much, he still can't stand it. Sometimes he feels comforted, as if Clem *is* there. Mainly he feels relief. It's so good to finally be talking and thinking about Clem with other people!

Carmen meets with the counselor every week. She notices that it continues to be different to talk to him. The first few times, she's just talking about Josh's death and how freaked out it makes her feel. Then, when she starts talking about her grandfather, she feels a lot of different things. Sometimes she cries, because she realizes that now she'll never have a chance to get to know her grandfather better. Maybe if he had lived until she was older, she wouldn't only have such bad memories of him. She also cries because she remembers how scared and lonely she felt when she was a little girl. At the time, she tried to be brave and not cry—so she cries now.

Also, though, Carmen finds herself feeling angry. "Why didn't my mom and dad know better what was going on with me?" she asks one day. "I was their kid! They should have noticed!" The counselor points out that Carmen's mother was probably so full of her own grief that she wasn't paying attention to Carmen.

"But I was just a little kid! She should have paid attention to me!" Carmen says.

"Yes, she should," the counselor agrees. "You were scared and you needed someone to explain things to you." Carmen feels so angry about what happened when she was younger that for a while, it's hard for her to be polite to her parents now. She's still so mad at them!

Later Carmen feels calmer about the whole thing—both her grandfather's death and Josh's. She starts to feel that she can go back to her regular life again, enjoying time with her friends and looking forward to going out with Roberto. She wonders, though, what she'd feel like if the people who died were closer to her than her grandfather and Josh were. "What if it was my mom, or my sister?" she says. "Or my dad? I couldn't stand it!"

The counselor says, "You could stand it. It might take you a whole lot longer to work through everything. But you *would* work through everything, Carmen, especially now, because now you understand that all your feelings are important, and you would take time to feel them all."

Losing People Whom We Love

Enduring the death of any loved one is painful and difficult. But different types of relationships involve different types of love—and raise different issues in the event of death. This chapter is about some specific issues that can come up when losing people in particular relationships.*

Losing a Parent

As we said earlier, the death of a parent is probably the most serious loss that a child or a teenager can face. Not only must the survivor endure the loss of a most beloved person, he or she also must face all the practical problems that follow. In a two-parent family, the teenager may have to deal with the family's financial hardship, with one parent doing the emotional and material work that two parents were doing before, perhaps with new people—other relatives or a housekeeper—coming into the household, and possibly having to move to another neighborhood or another town.

---

*For many of the insights in this chapter, we are indebted to Earl A. Grollman's *Straight Talk about Death for Teenagers*.

In a one-parent household, the young person who loses a parent must face the prospect of a new guardian as well as a new home, along with the question of where brothers and sisters will live. Teenagers in either situation may feel anxious or embarrassed about being different from their friends and classmates.

Another natural fear of teenagers who lose a parent is the prospect of remarriage. If the parent is lost after a prolonged illness, the remaining parent may already have established a relationship with someone that could lead to marriage. Even if this isn't the case, the teenager is aware that his or her parent probably is likely to start dating at some point. For young people who are just starting to date themselves, it can be especially upsetting to see a parent—who is supposed to be done with that part of life!—going through the same anxieties and adventures as the teenager. The teenager may feel that "Dating is *my* territory—marriage is yours! You don't belong here!" The teenager also may be upset at the idea of having to get used to yet another adult who's going to act like a parent. After all, the teen years aren't a time for becoming more dependent on parents—they're a time for breaking away!

On the other hand, if the remaining parent doesn't date or start new relationships, that also can be a strain. The teenager, in particular, can feel that he or she is supposed to take the place of the missing husband or wife. He or she may feel obligated to help the remaining parent with the family finances, to help talk out family problems, and generally to act like an adult partner, rather than to behave like a child who still needs to be taken care of. The remaining parent, consciously or unconsciously, may in fact be expecting this or even asking for it. The teenage girl with a widowed father may be asked to play the role of "little mother," cooking, cleaning, baby-sitting, and comforting her father. The teenage girl with a widowed mother may be asked to be "mom's best friend," supporting her mother emotionally as well as helping out around the house. Likewise, the teenage boy may be expected to be "the man around the house" or to become his dad's best buddy, the one his father can count on to "help with problems" and not to "*be* a problem."

In fact, it may be that a death in the family brings new responsibilities for all the children, and it's reasonable to expect teenagers to help out more. In fact, it is a time when teens can and do feel closer to their families. They have lived through the loss of a parent, and now see their surviving family members in a new light. This does not mean, however, that they must take on a totally new role. There's a fine line between helping out and becoming an adult before you're ready.

If you feel that the death of a parent has brought you more responsibilities than you can handle, you might talk about this with your remaining parent. Try to pick a time to bring this up when your parent has some free time, maybe even making the date in advance. ("I'd like to talk about some things around the house—would Saturday morning be a good time?") Bringing up your need to do less work while your mother is in the middle of cooking dinner, feeding the baby, and putting away the groceries is probably *not* going to get very good results!

If you feel that you're expected to do more housework, baby-sitting, and other chores than is reasonable, rather than simply protesting, you might try coming up with a plan for how much you *would* be willing to do, with suggestions for how the other work might get done. You might say something such as "I'm really worried about my grades, and I also feel like I never have time to see my friends. How would it be if, instead of watching the kids every day after school, I just baby-sat two times a week? Maybe we could do a baby-sitting exchange for one or two of the other times—I'll take Mrs. Battaglia's kids two days and she can take our kids the other two, and maybe we could afford a sitter for Fridays?" Or you might offer, "I don't mind cooking dinner three nights a week, but can we come up with some other plan for the other two nights? I really want to be on the swim team, but I can't if I have to come right home every single afternoon."

If you feel burdened emotionally, you might also try talking about that—again, picking a time when your parent can relax and when the two of you can have some privacy. You might say something such as "Mom, I know things are tough for you, but it makes me feel so bad when you tell me how lonely you are," or "Dad, when you tell me things aren't going well at work, I just don't know what to say."

If you're not happy with the response you get, or if you just can't face having this conversation in the first place, *get help.* Find an adult you trust—a relative, a teacher, a neighbor, a religious leader, a counselor—and get him or her to intervene. Your parent may need help coping with the death too—but you're still a teenager, not yet an adult. You can be loving, supportive, and helpful around the house without having to grow "all the way up" right away. (For more about getting help, see Chapters 6 and 7.)

A teenager who loses a parent may feel that he or she can't talk about the loss with the parent who remains. The remaining parent may be too grief-stricken to cope well, or the teenager may feel that the remaining parent is too fragile to share painful feelings with. After all, there's only one parent left now. Teenagers who have lost one parent may feel that they have to be extra careful to hang on to the one who remains.

If at all possible, we urge you and your parent to talk and cry about your loss together, along with any brothers and sisters you may have. At a time like this families need lots of time together as a group, as well as time to pair up, and time for everybody to be alone or with other friends. What often happens, though, is that people are afraid to share their grief with one another. If this is happening in your family, see if you can break the pattern. Make special times to be with each of your remaining family members, and think about organizing times for the whole family to be together.

If, for whatever reason, this is something you just can't do, see if you can find a sympathetic and trusted adult to connect to. Your teenage friends are very important right now, but you also need to be in touch with someone older, someone who has more perspective on what you're going through than a person of your own age. If you're not getting this kind of support from the parent you have left, find a way to get it from someone else.

Losing a Brother or Sister

Losing a brother or sister can be very hard on a teenager. A teenager who loses a sibling may feel that his or her very identity has changed. When someone asks, "How many brothers and sisters do you have?" what kind of answer will work for the teenager whose brother or sister has died? If the sibling who died was the only sibling, does that mean that the survivor is no longer a "brother" or a "sister," but simply an only child? What if before you weren't the oldest in your family—but now you are? Or maybe before you weren't the youngest—but what if you are now? Maybe you used to be in the middle, and now you're not there any more. It's a whole new identity to get used to.

Another hard part of losing a sibling is that, during the teen years especially, stormy relationships between siblings tend to exist. The teenager whose sibling dies may remember the fights and the competition—and will feel even more guilty and upset about the death. Of course, it's easy to say rationally that there's nothing to feel guilty about—all brothers and sisters fight, and all of them feel some amount of envy, resentment, and jealousy as well as love. When someone dies, though, our feelings often go to whatever was difficult in the relationship, as if that somehow caused the death. So the death of a teenager's brother or sister can hit pretty hard.

Yet it's easy for a teenager to be left out when a sibling dies, because many people will be focused on the grief of the parents. People seem to understand that parents feel terrible grief at the loss of a child. But if you've lost an older brother or sister, who understands that you may have lost someone you looked up to, someone who protected you, someone who ran interference for you with Mom and Dad (as well as someone who bossed you around and bullied you and got to do all the good stuff first!)? And if you've lost a younger brother or sister, does anyone realize that you've lost an admirer, someone you took care of, someone who thought you could do anything and who thought anything you did was more interesting than anything else in the world (as well as a pest and a tease and a chore to take care of!)?

It takes a long time to mourn a sibling. According to a 1981 study by D. E. Balk, cited by David Crenshaw in *Bereavement: Counseling the Grieving throughout the Life Cycle,* one-third to one-half of the teenagers interviewed reported that two years after the death, they were still feeling guilt, loneliness, depression, confusion, and anger. Yet many people may misunderstand the importance of this relationship, believing that the teen should "get over it" far sooner than is realistic.

Sometimes teenagers whose brother or sister has died feel that their parents or other family members expect them to take the sibling's place. If Johnny used to be the good student and Johnny dies, what happens to younger brother Ralph—does he have to fill Johnny's "good-student" shoes? If Lupe was a superfast runner and she dies, does Olga have to try out for the track team?

If you've lost a brother or sister and you're feeling pressure from your family to fill that person's space, we urge you to talk about this to someone. If it's at all possible, talk about it with your parents: "Now that Clem is gone, I feel like you want me to be like him" or "I miss Ed too, but you know, Sharon always used to ask *him* to help with her homework and now she asks me. It makes me feel weird."

If your parents are not receptive, or if you feel you can't talk about this with them, find another adult to talk about it with, maybe someone who will talk to your parents for you. As important as your friends are, you also need an older person to help you work through these problems—a relative, neighbor, family friend, religious leader, teacher, or counselor. (For more on getting help, see Chapters 6 and 7.) The best thing you can do for yourself at a time like this is to be aware of what you're feeling and to make sure you get what you need. That includes finding a grown-up who takes your feelings seriously.

Losing a Grandparent

Many teenagers' and children's first experiences with death come when they lose a grandparent. In some cases, the relationship with the grandparent was quite close. Then the death represents a real loss. The grandparent may have been someone who comforted the teenager, someone who was there just to talk to and hang out with when the parents were busy working or taking care of the house, someone who took the grandchild on special adventures or brought special presents. The grandparent may also have been somebody who took the grandchild's side against the parents once in a while, so that losing the grandparent feels like losing a special ally.

On the other hand, for many children, like Carmen, a grandparent might not be such a loving figure. Some grandparents are known to their grandchildren primarily as people who are old and sick, demanding and difficult, or simply not able to do much. The grandparents may not have gotten along well with *their* children, which may mean that their grandchildren felt the conflict and became un-comfortable. Some grandparents just aren't very good with children, or are good with little children but not with teenagers. Some don't understand that times have changed, or expect the same loyalty and obedience from their grandkids that they expected from their own children, which puts the grandchildren in a very difficult position.

It's also possible for children and teenagers not to have very much contact with their grandparents at all. Perhaps they live in a different city, or perhaps they rarely visit, even though they live quite close. Perhaps they stay in touch with their own children but not with their grandchildren.

Another complicating factor with grandparents is the way that parents feel about them. Most parents feel a mixture of love and frustration with *their* parents. Some parents quite actively dislike their own parents, or just don't get along with them. Some feel a lot of love but can't spend more than a couple of hours with their folks without arguing. Some, of course, enjoy their parents a great deal.

Whatever a parent's relationship to a grandparent, when the grandparent dies, it's likely to be extremely hard on the parent. Once again, this may be hard for a child or teenager. Everyone's sympathies are with the bereaved parent, and the child's needs may get lost in the shuffle. The child or teenager also may feel guilty or uncomfortable that Mom or Dad is so upset about an event that makes little difference to the younger generation. It's hard to realize, sometimes, that the death of your parent's *parent* means something quite different to him or her than what the death of your *grandparent* means to you.

If it's possible for you and the rest of your family to share your memories—good and bad—when a grandparent dies, that's wonderful. Sharing your grief—crying together, looking at photographs, or just sitting quietly with one another—can be a comforting and healing way to mourn.

If, on the other hand, your parents are still very angry with their parents, or if they are so overcome with grief that they aren't able to include you yet, find your own way to mourn your grandparent in the way that seems right for you. Write about the times you remember, both good and bad. Collect photographs of your ancestor and put them in an album, maybe adding a few lines of explanation or some other souvenirs of the person's life or of your shared life. Celebrate and grieve your own special relationship.

Losing a Friend

One of the hardest parts of losing a friend is how invisible the relationship may seem to others and how, therefore, there seems to be no place for a teenager's grief. Sometimes losing a friend is even more painful than losing a family member, and yet often there is no social space to mourn this loss. As Harry discovered, a friend may not even hear about a death until many days later. A friend may not be welcome at the funeral, or it just might not occur to either the family of the person who died or the survivor's family to take the time to acknowledge the friendship and its importance.

Sometimes the friend who dies was a boyfriend or girlfriend. In that case, the relationship may have been even more intense. It also may have been secret from one or both families, or, even if it was recognized, its intensity and importance may not be acknowledged. A teenager who loses a romantic partner may feel that his or her love is dismissed as "puppy love" or "going through a phase," rather than recognized as the truly important and heartfelt emotion that it was.

Teenagers with gay or lesbian attachments may feel even more displaced and ignored when a beloved friend dies. Not only may their relationship have been secret, the teenager may feel that he or she can't even talk about it honestly with friends, because of the negative way that many people in our society react to homosexuality.

In all these cases—losing a friend, losing a romantic partner, losing a gay or lesbian romantic partner—the pain and the loss that a teenager might feel are deep, intense, and legitimate. The challenge for a teenager in this situation is to find people with whom he or she can share feelings, memories, and tears, so that even if it takes some work, a space to mourn is created.

If you are in this situation, consider whether you want to organize your own memorial service with your friends, instead of, or as well as, going to the family's funeral or ceremony. Figure out which friends you can talk to openly and honestly about your relationship, and help them learn how to listen the way you need them to—ready to let you talk and remember, cry and be silent, laugh and distract yourself—without them needing to fix things for you or "make the pain go away." Help them understand that, as Earl A. Grollman puts it, you just have to hurt more now in order to hurt less later.

If you've had a gay or lesbian relationship and you don't know anyone you feel comfortable sharing that part of your grief with, see if you can find a gay or lesbian community center in your area, a gay rights group, or some other organization where there are people you can talk to freely and openly. You may also be able to find counselors in person or on a hot line who will accept your feelings and respect your grief. (For some suggestions, see Chapters 6 and 7.)

Relationships and Grief

A Texas researcher named Larry Bugen discovered that two factors seem to influence the intensity and duration of people's grief: how close they were to the person who died, and how much they felt that they could have prevented the death. If, for example, the person who died was killed while driving under the influence, and a friend gave him the keys to a car, that friend is likely to feel that he could probably have prevented the accident, and so feel a longer and more intense grief than the friend who was sitting home watching TV when the accident happened. On the other hand, the friend who was watching TV might also *feel,* rationally or not, that if only he had been out with his friend that night, *he* could have kept him from getting into the fatal car.

Getting clear about what we do and don't have control over is one of the things that death makes us deal with. Accepting that we usually *can't* prevent the death of another is one of the most painful parts of grief. But another painful part is recognizing that it's the very closeness of our relationship that has brought us pain. People who have been through the death of someone very close—a husband or wife, a child, a parent, a sibling, a friend or lover—say that the memories, the love—and the pain—are with them forever. Moving through grief has taught them to find a place for their pain along with their love.

In *Learning to Say Good-bye,* Eda LeShan puts it very well. She writes, "Most of all, I have learned that the pain never completely goes away, that there are always sudden piercing moments of grief—and that this is an indication of just how remarkably important and unique and wonderful people are. It would be far more terrible if our losses didn't matter." Or, to quote E. Schneidman (cited by Louis E. LaGrand in *Disenfranchised Grief*), "Grief is the ransom we pay for loving."

6

Getting Help

After Felicia's mother dies, Felicia's six-year-old brother Joey starts acting really badly. He can't stop teasing all of his friends at school—he keeps teasing them and taking their things away until they cry. Then he cries.

Meanwhile, Felicia's ten-year-old brother, Charles, seems to be handling everything okay, but he has started eating huge amounts of food. Plus, when Felicia goes to help her father clean out her mother's bedroom, they notice that some of her perfume bottles are missing. So are the pillows from her bed. They find those things in Charles's room.

Felicia's father must realize something is wrong, because one day he comes home and announces that the whole family is going together to see a family therapist. Felicia's father explains that they will all talk with this therapist about how they're feeling, and she'll help them deal with the death.

At first Felicia is so ashamed. No one she knows goes to see a therapist! Does this mean there's something really wrong with all of them?

After the first session, though, Felicia is relieved. Finally there's somebody who is willing to talk about what has happened! Even though Felicia's father still seems uncomfortable talking about his wife's illness and death, at least he lets the children talk while the therapist listens.

As Felicia's family continues to see the counselor, Felicia finds herself saying how upset and angry she is that her father never wanted to talk about what was happening. "It was so hard not knowing what was going on!" she says. "You told me not to ask Mom or even to talk to my friends. I felt like we had this terrible secret we couldn't share with anybody. And I couldn't even talk to you, and I wanted to."

Felicia's father's eyes fill with tears, but he doesn't say anything. Felicia realizes it may take a long time before he can talk to her openly, even with the counselor there. Maybe he'll never be able to do it. But at least now, she can talk about what she's feeling. And even though it hurts to let her mother go, it helps to have someone to talk to, and to talk and cry together as a family.

After the memorial service, things slowly start to get better for Harry. He still misses Clem, but he's finally able to enjoy times with his other friends—and now, because they've had the memorial service, he finds it easier to talk about Clem with them too.

One day in school, the English teacher asks the class to write about a person who has touched their lives. Harry finds himself writing about Clem. In his last paragraph, he writes, "I know now that no matter how many other great friends I have, I will never ever find another friend like Clem. There was just no one like him. But that's okay, because I did know him, and I will never forget him. And now whenever I think of him, it makes me sad to miss him, but it also makes me happy to remember that he was my friend."

Carmen feels that with the counselor's help, she is able to put Josh's death behind her and go on to enjoy her life. Then another tragedy happens. Carmen's teenage cousin

Luis is killed in the crossfire of a robbery that happened in a grocery store where he was picking up some bread and milk for his mother. It's just a freak accident—everybody thought that neighborhood was safe—and the shock seems to make the tragedy even worse.

Carmen feels very, very sad. She didn't know the cousin very well, but he was the son of her favorite aunt and uncle, and they feel terrible. So does the dead boy's brother, Mario, and Carmen does know him well, because he's closer to her age. Besides, Luis was so young! He had just started college, and he was doing so well—it's just not fair for him to die now.

Carmen cries a lot about Luis. She also feels very angry. She writes about her thoughts and feelings in a diary she started keeping while she was seeing the counselor. She also tells her friends about her cousin and shows them pictures from the family album. And she spends a lot of time at her aunt and uncle's house, helping them cook supper and helping Mario watch out for the three younger kids.

Carmen doesn't have any of her old fears, but sometimes it's still hard for her to sleep. And she knows that the pain of this death too will hurt her for a long time.

Accepting Help

As we've said several times already, this is a hard society in which to ask for and accept help. The dominant idea in American culture has always been "pulling yourself up by your bootstraps," "making it on your own," "being a self-made man (or woman)." The dominant hero has often been someone like John Wayne or Arnold Schwarzenegger—so big and tough that no one can hurt him in any way, either in his body or in his mind.

In such an atmosphere, it's hard to face the truth about grief: that it makes us feel vulnerable, that it may lead us to cry and to feel helpless, that it's not something we can properly go through alone. Precisely because someone else's death makes us realize how alone we really are, the time after a death is a time to reach out, to be with others, to share our feelings.

For many reasons, this may be hard for you or for someone you know to do. Perhaps, as with Harry, no one recognizes how important the death is to you. Perhaps, as with Carmen, an earlier death or loss is getting in the way of your reactions to the present. Or maybe, like Felicia, you have a family that isn't willing or able to talk and grieve openly and that for whatever reason is keeping you from working through your own grief.

In this case, our advice can be boiled down to two words: *Reach out.* Find as many people as you need—preferably both your own age and adults—whom you can talk to, cry with, or just be with. If you're lucky, you'll find friends who know how to handle grief, perhaps because they've been through a loss themselves. Or you may have to help people understand how to help you, telling them what you need—a shoulder to cry on, a listening ear, or a person to give you a hug, or hold you, or let you rant and rave. Help your teenage and adult friends understand that what you *don't* need is someone to tell you to cheer up, or someone who tells you why things really aren't so bad. What you *do* need is someone who can allow you to feel bad until you feel better. That's all it usually takes.

Deciding to Feel Better

But sometimes that's not *all* it takes. Sometimes a person can get stuck in grief. To use the language we suggested in Chapter 4, a person can get stuck in stage 2—expressing grief—and never move on to stage 3—understanding and accepting what has happened. Sooner or later everyone has to choose to recover, to feel better, in order to move on with his or her life. This may take a year or more, depending on how close the survivor was to the person who died—but sooner or later, everyone faces this decision. If you—or someone you know—feels that it's a decision that you're not able to make, you may need some help figuring out why, so you can resolve your feelings and move on.

Another reason that teenagers often need help with grief is because they get stuck in *depression* rather than in true *grieving*. Do you know the difference? Dr. Donna A. Gaffney explains it in *The Seasons of Grief: Helping Children Grow Through Loss.*

Depression is sadness plus anger, and it sometimes includes being angry at yourself; for example, "Why do I care so much about him anyway? This is stupid!" or "I'm such a terrible person—I don't deserve to be happy while she is lying dead in the ground!" A depressed person often feels tired, has trouble sleeping or sleeps too much, loses appetite or eats compulsively, and may also feel helpless and hopeless. Sometimes a depressed person will cover up his or her condition with a lot of frantic activity, but he or she will get no pleasure out of it.

A person who is *grieving,* on the other hand, may feel sad a lot, but he or she can sometimes switch to other moods, especially after the first week or two has passed. Although some difficulties with eating, sleeping, and energy level are normal—after all, grief takes up a lot of energy—the grieving people are able to eat, sleep, and exercise at a rate fairly close to normal. Although a grieving person may often be angry—at God, the person who died, the universe, or him- or herself—he or she can respond to warmth and reassurance, rather than feeling locked into the anger or feeling unable to be reached or to reach out. Even in the midst of sadness, a person who is grieving can sometimes find pleasure—in a good meal, a comfortable bed, a younger brother or sister's hug, a sweet song on the radio, a beautiful walk in the woods.

As you can see, it's not always easy to tell the difference between depression and grief. And it's normal to feel a certain amount of depression as part of the grieving process. If you feel that you or someone you know is locked into depression, though, it may be time to get help from a counselor or therapist who can help unlock buried feelings and allow the grieving process to continue more smoothly.

What Kinds of Help Are Available

Generally, a person who is dealing with grief will want to talk to a *counselor, therapist,* or *psychologist.* People in these professions have different types of degrees and background, but all are trained to talk to people about their problems and to help them find solutions by getting in touch with their feelings. (Your family doctor may also be a good person to talk with. She or he may be able to help you figure out your next step.)

Sometimes a religious leader—a priest, minister, or rabbi—can be a good counselor. Sometimes schools offer counselors. Or there may be a community center or youth center in your area that offers counseling services. Some counselors are specially trained to help people with problems of grief and mourning.

In some cases, it's helpful to talk to a *family therapist,* a person who is trained to work with an entire family. The family therapist's job is to help all family members speak together openly and honestly about their feelings. The idea is that if the family learns to communicate better, every member will be happier, in his or her own life and as part of the family.

Often grief is a family problem, so that one child or adult seems to "act out" while everyone else seems to "handle things well." In reality, though, everyone may be having a hard time with a death. It's just easier to let one person do all the acting out for everybody. A family therapist can help everyone realize that he or she has grief to deal with, and can help the family as a whole respect each of its members' ways of dealing with it.

Finding a Counselor

The first step for getting help is to talk to your parents. We urge you to do this if it's at all possible, because it's best if your parents can be involved in the help you're getting. You might remember that Harry's parents, for example, were able to suggest some things that Harry could do once they were aware of his problem. And when Felicia's father went with her to see a therapist, she felt she could talk to him more easily, which immediately made her feel better.

Sometimes, though, it's just not possible to talk to your parents about getting help; or, if you do bring up the subject, they may not be receptive. In that case, we urge you to *keep trying. Don't give up!* Here are some other suggestions for getting the help you need:

- **Ask a friend.** Maybe someone you know is already seeing a counselor or therapist and can give you that person's phone number. Although you may not be able to afford the counselor's fee, he or she may be able to help you find one that you can afford.
- **Ask an adult you trust.** A relative, a favorite teacher, a religious leader, or just someone you know may be able to point you in the right direction or even suggest someone to see.
- **Ask at school.** Maybe there's a school counselor who can either counsel you or help you find the right kind of counseling. Maybe the school nurse knows how to proceed. Perhaps you can find resources listed in the school library.
- **Look in the yellow pages.** Try "Social Services," "Counseling," "Therapy," and "Psychologists." Write down any number that looks promising and when you call, explain

what you're looking for. Asking someone to help you find a counselor—even if he or she is not the one—is called *getting a referral.*

- **Look at Chapter 7 of this book.** Maybe there's a hot line or organization in your state or community that can be a starting point for you to get help.

Coming to Terms with Death

Learning how to deal with grief, facing the mysteries of death and dying, coping with the pain of letting a loved one go while you remain—these are normal but painful realities of the human condition that no one has solved. If you are having to face them as a teenager, or if you had to face them as a child, you are coming to them at a younger age than most people. This is a terrible journey to have to make so young—but it can also offer you a kind of bittersweet opportunity.

As we've said, no one ever to totally "resolves" the grief that comes from losing a beloved person. You can't hope for the "missing you" feeling to disappear forever. But what you can hope is that your feelings and memories about the person you lost will become a source of strength and comfort in your life, along with whatever longing they still have the power to bring. The pain, however, will go away.

As R. Meryman put it in an interview with B. Stein in the April 20, 1981 issue of *People* magazine:

> Successful grief . . . is really coming out better than you went in. It's coming out enriched and a better person because you have lived through all of that pain, because you have assessed your life, assessed your [relationship to the person who died], and assessed yourself. You become more sympathetic with people and have a greater joy in you. You sense the preciousness of time. You are focused on what is important. In sum, you not only survive; you are much more alive.

7

Where to Find
Help

The following organizations will be able to provide you with referrals and advice in dealing with a variety of issues related to dealing with death and dying.

Death and Dying

Center for Loss and Life Transitions
3735 Broken Arrow Road
Fort Collins, CO 80526
303-226-6050
This organization offers comprehensive services to those who have experienced loss, including clinical care and education for those who have lost loved ones, as well as training for those who work with the bereaved.

Family Service Association of America
44 East 23rd Street
New York, NY 10010

Helping families to cope with stress—including the stress caused by a death in the family—is the mission of this organization.

Grief Education Institute
2422 South Downing Street
Denver, CO 80210
This institute offers support groups and individual counseling for the bereaved, as well as seminars, public education programs, and workshops for people in the helping professions.

Make Today Count
P.O. Box 222
Osage Beach, MO 65065
This international organization has local chapters nationwide to support people with life-threatening illnesses.

National Mental Health Association
1021 Prince Street
Alexandria, VA 22314-2971
703-684-7722
This group provides information about grief, bereavement, and other issues that relate to losing a loved one.

National Center for Death Education
777 Dedham Street
Newton Centre, MA 02159
617-928-4649
This library and resource center offers workshops and continuing education programs as well as providing books, films, and other materials about death, dying, and bereavement.

Additional Resources

The following organizations can provide you with referrals and advice in dealing with problems that may be related to coping with serious illness, death, or dying.

Suicide and Homicide

Families of Homicide Victims Groups
The Village for Families and Children
c/o Lillian Serrano
1680 Albany Avenue
Hartford, CT 06105
203-297-0541

Survivors of Homicide Support Group
State of Connecticut
Office of Victim Services
1155 Silas Deane Highway
Wethersfield, CT
203-529-3089
This agency offers periodic support groups under the direction of trained professionals, as well as mutual support and self-help groups for families who have lost a member through murder, as well as referrals for free individual counseling.

The Families of Homicide Victims Program
Victim Services Agency
2 Lafayette Street
New York, NY 10007
212-834-6688
This agency provides counseling, crisis support, specialized services, and help in getting financial aid for those who have lost a loved one to violence.

Ray of Hope, Inc.
P.O. Box 2323
Iowa City, IA 52244
A group for those who have lost a loved one through suicide, this agency provides telephone counseling, support services, printed resources, videotapes, and, in some cases, speakers and presentations.

Seasons: Suicide Bereavement
4777 Nanilos Drive
Salt Lake City, UT 84117
This national organization has many local chapters dedicated to helping those who have lost a loved one through suicide.

Suicide Awareness: Voices of Education (SAVE)
5124 Grove Street
Minneapolis, MN 55436
612-946-7998
A group whose publications and presentations are directed at both friends and families of suicide victims.

Suicide Prevention Center, Inc.
P.O. Box 1393
Dayton, OH 45401
513-297-4777
This group is a volunteer crisis line that offers support over the phone. They can also refer you to information about discussions, newsletters, telephone referrals, educational programs, and presentations aimed at helping friends and families of suicide victims.

Alcohol and Drug Problems

Al-Anon Family Group Headquarters
1372 Broadway
New York, NY 10036
212-302-7240

See the white pages for the group in your area. Al-Anon helps those over the age of 13 deal with alcohol problems in their families.

Alcoholics Anonymous (A.A.) World Services
475 Riverside Drive
New York, NY 10115
212-870-3400
See the white pages for the A.A. group in your area. This organization provides free assistance for those seeking recovery from alcohol problems.

Narcotics Anonymous World Services Office
16155 Wyandotte Street
Van Nuys, CA 91406
818-780-3951
This organization provides general reference services for those seeking recovery from narcotics addiction.

National Cocaine Hotline
1-800-262-2463
This service helps cocaine users, their friends, and their families.

Pills Anonymous Hotline
212-874-0700
This group offers support for people with drug dependency problems.

Sexually Transmitted Diseases

Centers for Disease Control National HIV and AIDS Hotline
English-language line (24 hours):
1-800-342-2437

Spanish-language line (8AM-2AM):
1-800-344-7432

Line for the Deaf (TTY line, 10AM-10PM):
1-800-243-7889
A toll-free phone call can provide answers to questions
about HIV and AIDS.

CHOICE Hotline
215-985-3300
This help line answers teenagers' questions about sexually
transmitted diseases, AIDS, birth control, pregnancy, abor-
tion, prenatal care and other related topics. Spanish operators available.

Gay Men's Health Crisis AIDS Hotline
212-807-6655
This hot line provides information about AIDS; it is part of
Gay Men's Health Crisis, an activist organization that provides a wide range of services to people with AIDS and
their loved ones. Spanish operators available.

Gay and Lesbian Support Groups

The Bridges Project of the American Friends Service
Committee
1501 Cherry Street
Philadephia, PA 19102
215-241-7133
This group provides information and referrals for gay and
lesbian youth and youth service providers.

Gay and Lesbian Switchboard of New York, Inc.
212-777-1800
This hot line provides a guide to resources relating to gay
and lesbian issues. It's available 7 days a week from 10 a.m.
to midnight. You can either talk to a volunteer or get
information from an automated phone service.

National Center for Lesbian Rights Public Policy Office
462 Broadway
New York, NY
212-343-9589

870 Market Street, Suite 570
San Francisco, CA 94102
415-392-6257
or:
1-800-528-6257
This national organization is a clearinghouse for information about all aspects of lesbian life.

New York City Gay & Lesbian Anti-Violence Project, Inc.
647 Hudson
New York, NY 10014
(24-hour hot line):
212-807-0197
This is a resource, support, and action group for the targets of antigay violence.

Parents and Friends of Lesbians and Gays
212-463-0629
This organization is a support and information group for the families and friends of gay people.

For Further Reading

The following books will provide further information on death and dying.

Berry, Joy. *About Death*. Chicago: Children's Press, 1990.

Bratman, Fred. *Everything You Need to Know When a Parent Dies*. New York: The Rosen Group, 1992.

Buckman, Robert. *I Don't Know What to Say: How to Help and Support Someone Who Is Dying*. New York: Random House, 1988.

Colgrove, Melba, Harold H. Bloomfield, and Peter McWilliams. *How to Survive the Loss of a Love*. Los Angeles: Prelude Press, 1991.

DiGiulio, Robert. *After Loss*. Waco, TX: WRS Publishing, 1993.

Fayerweather Street School Staff. *The Kids' Book About Death and Dying*. Boston: Little, Brown & Company, 1985.

Gravelle, Karen, and Charles Haskins. *Teenagers Face to Face with Bereavement*. New York: Simon & Schuster, 1989.

Greenlee, Sharon. *When Someone Dies*. Atlanta: Peachtree Publishers, 1992

Grollman, Earl A. *Straight Talk About Death for Teenagers: How to Cope with Losing Someone You Love*. Boston: Beacon Press, 1993.

———. *Talking about Death: A Dialogue between Parent and Child*. Boston: Beacon Press, 1990.

Heegard, Marge E. *Coping with Death and Grief*. Minneapolis: Lerner Publications Company, 1990.

Hyde, Margaret O. *Meeting Death*. New York: Walker & Company, 1989.

James, John W., and Frank Cherry. *The Grief Recovery Handbook: A Step-by-Step Program for Moving beyond Loss*. New York: Harper & Row, 1988.

Knox, Jean. *Death and Dying.* New York: Chelsea House Publishers, 1989.

Kübler-Ross, Elisabeth, *Death: The Final Stage of Growth.* New York: Simon & Schuster, 1975.

———. *On Children and Death.* New York: Macmillan, 1983.

———. *On Death and Dying.* New York: Macmillan, 1969.

LeShan, Eda. *Learning to Say Good-bye: When a Parent Dies.* New York: Macmillan, 1976.

Levin, Stephen. *A Gradual Awakening.* New York: Doubleday, 1989.

Lightner, Candy, and Nancy Hathaway. *Giving Sorrow Words: How to Cope with Grief and Get On with Your Life.* New York: Time Warner, 1990.

Manning, Doug. *Don't Take My Grief Away.* San Francisco: Harper & Row, 1984.

McGuire, Leslie. *Death and Illness.* Vero Beach, FL: Rourke Corporation, 1990.

Pringle, Laurence. *Death Is Natural.* New York: William Morrow & Company, 1991.

Raab, Robert A. *Coping with Death.* Rev. ed. New York: The Rosen Publishing Group, 1989.

Stein, Sara B. *About Dying: An Open Family Book for Parents and Children Together.* New York: Walker & Company, 1984.

Stewart, Gail. *Death.* New York: Macmillan Children's Book Group, 1989.

Tatelbaum, Judy. *The Courage to Grieve: Creative Living, Recovery, and Growth Through Grief.* New York: Harper & Row, 1980.

INDEX